*Cultural Transactions*

# Cultural Transactions

## NATURE, SELF, SOCIETY

---

## Paul Hernadi

## Cornell University Press

*Ithaca and London*

First published 1995 by Cornell University Press.

*Library of Congress Cataloging-in-Publication Data*

Hernadi, Paul, 1936–
    Cultural transactions : nature, self, society / Paul Hernadi.
        p.   cm.
    Includes bibliographical references and index.
    ISBN 0–8014–3113–1
    1. Communication and culture.   2. Interpersonal communication.
    I. Title.
    P94.6.H47   1995
    302.2—dc20                                                    95–6968

Printed in the United States of America

♾ The paper in this book meets the minimum requirements
of the American National Standard for Information Sciences—
Permanence of Paper for Printed Library Materials, ANSI Z39.48-1984.

# Contents

CONTENTS

# Preface and Acknowledgments

This book explores the interplay of nature, self, and society in cultural transactions—the intertwined acts of doing, making, and meaning from which human worlds emerge. I sketched an outline for the book about eight years ago but recall working toward it ever since I began trying to pull things together as a precocious teenager in the 1950s. The range of things to be pulled together has of course been expanding over the years, and so has the circle of stimulating teachers, colleagues, and students with whom I have had the privilege of exchanging notes in several countries and various disciplines.

To retrace my academic itinerary, I studied mainly music and Hungarian literature in Budapest, mainly theater, English literature, and philosophy in Vienna, and mainly comparative literature (including the history and theory of criticism) at Yale. Later on I taught mainly German at Colorado College and the University of Rochester and mainly English at the University of Iowa and the University of California, Santa Barbara. Meanwhile, I have also come into fruitful contact with additional fields of humanistic inquiry as a resident fellow at the Wesleyan Center for the Humanities, as the executive secretary of the Midwest Modern Language Association, as the director of the Interdisciplinary Humanities Center at the University of California, Santa Barbara, and as the editor of four multiauthor books and two special issues of journals: *What Is Literature?*, *What Is Criticism?*, *The Horizon of Literature*, *The Rhetoric of Interpretation and the Interpretation of Rhetoric*, *More Ways of Worldmaking*, and *Objective, Subjective, Intersubjective Times*.

Having engaged in such activities, I owe much of what is well informed and valuable in this book to far more people than I can list here. I owe a special debt, however, to five friends and colleagues who offered detailed comments after reading earlier versions of the ensuing pages. Even in the age of telefax and electronic mail, it seems easiest to pressure local folks—with whom you have more or less regular lunch, chess, or tennis dates—into such self-sacrifice. Thank you, Chuck Bazerman, Ed Branigan, Wally Chafe, and Don Guss, and many thanks, once again, Bert States! I am also grateful to Jeffrey Sturges for years of reliable research assistance and for helping to prepare the index.

About one-ninth of the book has been previously published. In particular the first, second, and fourth sections of Chapter 1 closely follow the argument presented in "Doing, Making, Meaning: Toward a Theory of Verbal Practice," *PMLA* 103 (October 1988): 749–58. Some minor borrowing of additional ideas, phrases, or sentences is acknowledged in the notes that refer to my articles in four journals (*ADE Bulletin*, *Critical Inquiry*, *Journal of Aesthetic Education*, and *Time and Society*) and two books (*The Rhetoric of the Human Sciences: Language and Argument in Scholarship and Human Affairs*, ed. John S. Nelson, Allan Megill, and Donald N. McCloskey, and *Visionary Poetics: Essays on Northrop Frye's Criticism*, ed. Robert D. Denham and Thomas Willard). There is very little overlap with my earlier books, *Beyond Genre: New Directions in Literary Classification* and *Interpreting Events:*

viii

*Tragicomedies of History on the Modern Stage,* both published by Cornell University Press. But I am equally grateful to Bernhard Kendler and others at the Press for their help on those books and on this one, which I dedicate to Virginia and Christopher on this August 18, 1994—our thirtieth wedding anniversary and his twenty-fourth birthday.

PAUL HERNADI

*Santa Barbara, California*

*Cultural Transactions*

# Prologue: Enticements and Forewarnings

This book approaches culture, existence, and experience as elongated, overlapping shadows of three familiar activities: doing, making, and meaning. The shadows are elongated because culture, existence, and experience—our ways of being with, of, and toward a radically plural world—surpass particular acts of doing, making, and meaning. And the shadows overlap because human beings concurrently do, make, and mean things as players of socially assigned roles, as productive and reproductive organisms, and as self-conscious persons.

Doing, making, meaning; ways of being with, of, and toward the world; overlapping shadows. Why resort to such plain language—some might call it baby talk—at our advanced stage of terminological maturity? I am not allergic to technical terms. Nor am I reluctant to switch on (mostly in the notes that a hurried reader may decide to ignore) some high-powered searchlights that theorists since Plato have trained on everyday phenomena. But I find the current idiom of much humanistic inquiry more removed from ordinary speech than I think it ought or has to be. This state of affairs often keeps us from productively affirming or criticizing what familiar words prompt us to do, make, and mean. My ensuing affirmations and criticisms are designed to be therapeutic, even self-healing. For example, I hope that the discussion in chapter 3 of saying "we" may give both you and me the cautious confidence to speak, write, and think of "us"—a much maligned but insufficiently understood pronoun—without defensive quotation marks. In other chapters too, I try to remove blinkers that prevent culture, existence, and experience from coming into view as complementary horizons of social activity, natural facticity, and personal identity.

The resolutely three-dimensional approach should help my book outgrow what it grows out of: the current intersubjectivist bias in the humanities and social sciences. For many centuries people viewed either matter or mind—either nature or spirit—as the ultimate principle of all being and becoming. In contrast, a great deal of recent thinking stipulates the "social construction of reality."[1] I recognize the world-making and self-making powers of language and other vehicles of culture but also wish to heed the material conditions and personal responsibilities associated with the exercise of such powers. After all, even face-to-face verbal communication—a quintessentially intersubjective process— is simultaneously geared to personal identity, social activity, and natural facticity whenever an *I* talks to at least one of *you* about one or more of *them*. Such interplay of first-, second-, and third-person orientations at the very heart of intersubjectivity suggests that no circumspect understanding of culture, let alone of existence or experience, can be based on the study of social activity alone. Seen against the second-person horizon of intersubjective activity, human beings emerge as players of social roles. Against

1. I borrow the quoted phrase from the title of Peter L. Berger and Thomas Luckmann, *The Social Construction of Reality: A Treatise in the Sociology of Knowledge* (New York: Anchor-Doubleday, 1967).

the respective horizons of third-person facticity and first-person identity, they emerge as natural organisms and personal selves.[2]

To be sure, we typically experience ourselves at any particular time in just one of three ways: as objectively existing organisms, as players of intersubjectively assigned and evaluated roles, or as subjective selves. Yet we should, I think, avoid elevating one type of experience into a master doctrine that debunks the other two as mere delusions. Exclusive concern for only one strain in the texture of our lives easily leads to dubious totalizing claims like "It's all in the genes," "Individuals are mere products of their society," or "Every person is a fully autonomous moral agent." The undeniable appeal of each such tenet stems from its capacity to permit its adherents to deal with one, and repress two, of three profoundly troubling aspects of being human—death, interdependence, and responsibility. It is true that acknowledging just one dimension of our threefold plight can provide temporary relief from anxieties linked to the other two. By contrast, accepting each set of constraints associated with our lives as organisms, role-players, and selves imposes on us the task of staring down three predicaments rather than just one: natural (or supernatural) determination, social coercion, and personal conscience. The task is hard, yet recognizing all three predicaments seems to be required for achieving viable degrees of existential congruence, cultural consensus, and experiential coherence in our postmodern worlds.

2. There is growing recognition of the three-dimensionality of being human. For tripartite approaches comparable to mine, see Jürgen Habermas, *The Theory of Communicative Action*, vol. 1, *Reason and Rationalization of Society*, trans. Thomas McCarthy (Boston: Beacon, 1984), esp. pp. 10, 16, 45, 52, 69–75, 100, 278, and 308 on subjective, objective, and intersubjective (or social) "world relations," and Rom Harré's recently completed "trilogy": *Social Being: A Theory for Social Psychology* (Totowa, N.J.: Rowman and Littlefield, 1980), *Personal Being: A Theory for Individual Psychology* (Cambridge: Harvard University Press, 1984), and *Physical Being: A Theory for Corporeal Psychology* (Oxford: Blackwell, 1991). My own approach is quite different, however. For example, neither Habermas nor Harré suggests that the subjective, objective, and intersubjective (or the personal, physical, and social) are reciprocally constitutive dimensions of each other or that culture, existence, and experience interface in a utopian "we"-perspective of intertwined diversity.

The diversity of human worlds gives rise to many conceptual schemes without being encompassed by any. It is indeed tempting to insist that the multiple worlds shaped by our physically, socially, and mentally inhabiting them do not constitute a single world.[3] But such insistence is more unitarian than it appears because it surreptitiously implies the privileged existence, after all, of *a* particular world in which the notion of *the* world is "well lost."[4] To avoid deluding myself and my readers about this kind of trap, I often refer to the world(s)—which I view and discuss as more than one pluriverse—in the singular. The inconsistency involved might have pleased Friedrich Schlegel, who noted almost two hundred years ago: "It is equally lethal for the mind to have a system and to have none. It may very well have to decide to combine the two."[5]

I cited Schlegel's aphorism in two earlier books,[6] but my work on the present one has even more urgently required me to keep in mind the shrewd romantic ironist's paradoxical message. I hope that Schlegel's protopostmodern advice has helped me once again to stay alert both to the life-sustaining force of theoretical systems and to their self-induced decadence. To be more specific, this book intertwines several triadic sets of conceptual coordinates, some of which destabilize each other. I thus attempt to meet the

3. See the section titled "The Many Worlds" in chapter 21 of William James, *The Principles of Psychology*, 2 vols. (New York: Dover, 1950), 2:291–93. This edition is a reprint of the 1890 edition published by Henry Holt.
4. See Nelson Goodman, "The Way the World Is," *Review of Metaphysics* 14 (1960): 48–56; Richard Rorty, "The World Well Lost," *Journal of Philosophy* 69 (1972): 649–65; and Nelson Goodman, *Ways of Worldmaking* (Indianapolis: Hackett, 1978).
5. In the original, the fifty-third of Schlegel's "Athenaeum Fragments" (1798) reads: "Es ist gleich tödlich für den Geist, ein System zu haben, und keins zu haben. Er wird sich also wohl entschließen müssen, beides zu verbinden." Quoted from Friedrich Schlegel, *Kritische Schriften und Fragmente*, 6 vols., ed. Ernst Behler and Hans Eichner (Padeborn: Schöningh, 1988), 2:109. For a somewhat different English version, see Friedrich Schlegel, *Lucinde and the Fragments*, trans. Peter Firchow (Minneapolis: University of Minnesota Press, 1971), p. 167.
6. Paul Hernadi, *Beyond Genre: New Directions in Literary Classification* (Ithaca: Cornell University Press, 1972), p. 2, and idem, *Interpreting Events: Tragicomedies of History on the Modern Stage* (Ithaca: Cornell University Press, 1985), p. 11.

4

mind's demand for both having and not having a system by way of arguments whose dialectical "marriage of heaven and hell"— to invoke William Blake, another ironic romanticist—simultaneously procreates and devours all "portions" of the "whole."[7]

To give a capsule summary of what lies ahead: Chapter 1 pleads for approaching all discourse (whether oral, written, or mental) as concurrent doing, making, and meaning. Chapter 2 amplifies the initial conceptual framework by extending it to cover the performance, recording, and mental rehearsal of nonverbal communication, expression, and representation as well. Chapter 3 explores how the first-, second-, and third-person horizons of our potential for being active, receptive, and represented participants in cultural transactions can be fused into the shared identity of "we"-sayers. Chapter 4 attempts to shed light on the intertwined social, natural, and personal evolutions that have enabled us to emerge as (inter)active role-players, (re)productive organisms, and (self) conscious individuals. Chapter 5 both relates and contrasts my conceptions of culture, existence, and experience to three time-honored triads—the rhetorical aims of moving, delighting, and teaching, the psychological capacities of willing, feeling, and knowing, and the evaluative criteria of justice, beauty, and truth.

The brief Epilogue presents a few afterthoughts in a conversation about some of the book's loose ends. One of the critical voices raised likens the study as a whole to the Escher sketch of two hands drawing each other.[8] Let me expand on that remark

---

7. See esp. plate 16 in William Blake, *The Marriage of Heaven and Hell* (New York: Oxford University Press, 1975), p. xxiii: "One portion of being is the Prolific, the other the Devouring; to the devourer it seems as if the producer was in his chains; but it is not so, he only takes portions of existence and fancies that the whole."

8. See *Escher on Escher: Exploring the Infinite*, trans. Karin Ford (New York: Abrams, 1989), p. 66, where the Dutch artist remarks: "Some years after I made this print I saw exactly the same idea of two hands drawing each other in a book by the famous American cartoonist Saul Steinberg." This reference is probably to Saul Steinberg, *The Passport* (London: Hamish Hamilton, 1954), [p. 23], lower left corner. For some reason the 1978 edition of *The Passport* does not include the drawing in question.

and on Escher's image of reciprocal self-articulation as follows. My chief aspirations have indeed been (1) to show that culture, existence, and experience are the social, natural, and personal dimensions of each other and (2) to prompt critical readers to draw my drawing hand into their evolving systems and nonsystems. We certainly need a lot of hands as we try to piece together today's cultural, existential, and experiential puzzles. More often than not, doing so requires us to combine having and not having a system—to intertwine the diverse without reducing the diversity of the intertwined.

*Chapter One*

# How to Do, Make, and Mean Things with Words

Speech and writing, the two principal means of communication in literate societies, closely link discourse to doing and making. We conspicuously do something whenever we engage in vocal interaction with at least one other person, and we conspicuously make something whenever we produce a text for future use or contemplation.[1] If we mouth or copy words without understanding them, doing or making is all there is to it. But if we comprehend the discourse that we utter or inscribe, we not only do or make but also mean something. Moreover, we need not speak or

---

1. Since speech is the most typical form of verbal doing, it is not surprising that John Austin was mainly interested in the *doing* of things with *spoken* words. See J. L. Austin, *How to Do Things with Words* (1962), 2d ed. (Cambridge: Harvard University Press, 1975). Austin's memorable title and his sharp but narrow primary focus on utterances are expanded in the title and concerns of this chapter. It is worth noting at the outset that acts of face-to-face communication are possible without voiced utterances (e.g., through a sign language or the exchange of written notes), and that tape recorders and movie cameras have recently joined writing in preserving oral speech acts for subsequent reproduction. Much more will be said about such matters in the next chapter.

7

write in order to mean; we do so whenever we grasp the sense of words that we hear or read. And we can mean even without hearing or reading words as long as we think verbally enough to know which words, if heard or read, would express our thoughts.[2] In short, speaking, writing, and quasi-verbal thinking gear discourse, as something preeminently done or made or meant, toward action, production, or signification.[3]

## Action, Production, Signification

In the next section of this chapter I address the close and important ties between speaking and verbal action, between writing and verbal production, and between thinking and quasi-verbal signification. Here I want to stress that all discourse (whether spoken, written, or mental) evolves in all three dimensions. The following simple examples illustrate the constant interplay of doing, making, and meaning in the various ways we use words.

2. See Nelson Goodman, *Of Minds and Other Matters* (Cambridge: Harvard University Press, 1984), p. 24: "Thinking in words or pictures may often involve preparing or being ready not, or not only, to produce such words or pictures but rather, or also, to judge a word or picture produced or presented as agreeing or not agreeing with the one in mind."

3. Not all languages make as clear a distinction as we find in English between making and doing. For example, German *machen* often stands in for *tun* in colloquial contexts, and French *faire* carries the double semantic burden alone. Even in idiomatic English the semantic borderline between the two verbs is far from precise: Why is it that we make money but do a job, make love but do a favor? Many common idioms do reinforce, however, the English speaker's semantic assumption that whatever has been made—an impression, a promise, a law, an exception—will stay done for a while. In short, we expect that most making will, in principle, produce lasting effects. Such an expectation arises whether or not our native tongue or a language we know well happens to give us distinct verbs like "make" and "do" for distinguishing between two orientations of human behavior: one toward creation or production, the other toward action or interaction. Likewise, we can become and remain aware that making is a special kind of doing whether or not we realize that such different languages as German, ancient Greek, and Hungarian permit their equivalent of "make" (*machen, poein, csinálni*) to be used in a secondary sense corresponding to "do" (*tun, prattein, tenni*) but not vice versa.

8

Consider first the speech events occurring at a murder trial. Every verbal "thing done" in the courtroom (like uttering a sworn testimony or reading aloud a guilty verdict) is part of an ongoing action in which the participants perform mutually recognized speaker and listener roles (such as the roles of defendant, witness, juror, judge, or spectator). But each intersubjective act of speech makes subjective minds contemplate whatever the speaker is talking about (for example, a smoking gun in the alleged killer's hand), and it can also bring about certain events in the objective world of jails and electric chairs.[4] Similar interconnections characterize discourse in its written guise as a thing made. Every text (say, the original manuscript of a Wordsworth poem or a humble Help Wanted sign in a shop window) is a verbal "thing made"— the objectively existing product of an instance of inscribing. But any objective inscription can prompt varied subjective construals and thus lead to different degrees of intersubjective communication between the senders and receivers of messages. Finally, every quasi-verbal thought is a mental "thing" more obviously meant than made or done. But what you subjectively think (for instance, about your next-door neighbor's being dishonest) is tied to intersubjective formations (for example, gossip) and may lead to objectively consequential behavior (an obvious case would be the mental act of deciding how to burn down your neighbor's house). In other words, whenever we "say" something—whether in speech, in writing, or in silent deliberation[5]—we potentially do or undo, make or destroy, and mean or repress something at the same time.

4. The fourth section of this chapter should clarify the sense in which I both distinguish and interrelate subjective, objective, and intersubjective aspects of discourse and of human life throughout the book.

5. The conversational nature of thought processes was already noted by Plato's Socrates, who called solitary deliberation "the conversation which the soul holds with herself" (*Theaetetus* 189–90 in Jowett's translation); see also Plato's *Sophist* 263–64, where the same view is expressed twice by the wise Stranger from Elea. (For all Plato references I use *The Dialogues of Plato*, trans. B. Jowett, 2 vols. [1892; New York: Random House, 1937].) In much more recent

9

Now, our doing, making, and meaning things with words relies on the profound interdependence of intersubjective activity, objective facticity, and subjective identity. Indeed, verbal practice constantly reveals that human culture, existence, and experience jointly emerge from what thereby becomes a dialectical interplay of the cultural, natural, and personal aspects of our lives. Whoever speaks, writes, or thinks does so, simultaneously, as the performer of a socially assigned role (for instance, the consulting patient or the happy prizewinner), as a biological organism (capable of responding predictably to environmental stimuli) and as a distinct person who self-consciously experiences a certain biological or social event (for instance, a toothache or an awards ceremony) in a specific way. Even the evolutionary process to which we owe our inborn capacity for language has wound its way through rudimentary practices of first prehuman, then human, communication among increasingly self-aware individuals.[6] On the one hand, individuals can speak, write, and think today because they are members both of the human species and of a particular language community. On the other hand, the biological and social baggage we individually carry would be different had our countless forebears not made their own individual contributions, however small, to the evolution of the human species in and through the histories of particular societies.

Regarded as action, discourse is both an instance of doing and a thing done: it is motivated by competitive or collaborative desire, and it can motivate competitive or collaborative desire. Regarded as production (or, if you like, creation), discourse is both a process of making and a thing made on at least two counts. It be-

---

works, Lev Vygotsky and Mikhail Bakhtin stressed the social origin of individual thinking conceived as internalized dialogue. See the informative juxtaposition of comparable statements by the two Russians in Caryl Emerson, "The Outer Word and Inner Speech: Bakhtin, Vygotsky, and the Internalization of Language," *Critical Inquiry* 10 (1983): 245–64.

6. See below, esp. the third section, as well as the second section of chapter 4.

comes part of the world's physical makeup: the speaker produces sound waves, the writer produces marks on paper. It also adds to the world's ideological makeup: where would Cinderella be, or even Lincoln as we know him, without the fictive and historical world-making of discourse? Regarded as signification, discourse is both an event of meaning and a thing meant: it articulates inchoate experience into conveyable information.

In the conjunctive view presented in this chapter and further elaborated in the next, spoken, written, and mental discourses alike have a transactive, an objective, and an experiential dimension. There is nothing wrong with focusing on just one of the three pairs of cultural practice in which discourse is typically encountered: speaking and listening, writing and reading, occurring and recalling.[7] But the close physiological links between those audible, visible, and mental guises of verbal discourse should also be kept in mind. The writing and reading of texts—as well as the reading, so to speak, of one's own mind while it is engaged in quasi-verbal thinking—are routinely accompanied by incipient movements of our speech muscles and probably also by

7. Literary critics cluster in three groups according to whether they approach literature mainly as a field of verbal transactions, as a set of verbal objects, or as a pool of occasions for quasi-verbal experience. Members of the first group, for whom literature is primarily action rather than production or signification, seem to assume that face-to-face oral utterances are exemplary of all discourse. Members of the second group, who tend to compare verbal constructs to things like "well-wrought urns," take texts as their paradigm for literary discourse. The third group in turn stresses the reader's literary experience rather than the verbal transactions or verbal objects that have triggered that experience. New historicism, (American) new criticism, and reader response criticism are relatively recent critical schools respectively exemplifying the three orientations just mentioned. But some of the best teachers and pupils in each "school" (e.g., Stephen Greenblatt, Cleanth Brooks, and Wolfgang Iser) often pay almost equal attention to what is done, made, and meant with words. See, for instance, Stephen Greenblatt, *Shakespearean Negotiations: The Circulation of Social Energy in Renaissance England* (Berkeley and Los Angeles: University of California Press, 1988); Cleanth Brooks, *The Well-Wrought Urn: Studies in the Structure of Poetry* (New York: Reynal, 1947); and Wolfgang Iser, *Prospecting: From Reader Response to Literary Anthropology* (Baltimore: Johns Hopkins University Press, 1989).

the incipient activation of our hearing organs.[8] Such involuntary "doing" anchors the "making" of texts and the "meaning" of quasi-verbal thoughts within the same few cubic inches of the human body where the audible uttering of words also occurs.

The analyzer of a particular verbal message may, of course, approach it as principally one kind of "thing" rather than another: something done (in the intersubjective realm of social roles), something made (in the objective domain of natural entities or in the domain of the "objective contents of thought")[9], or something meant (by a self-conscious embodiment of individual subjectivity). Furthermore, the view that all discourse is simultaneously action, production, and signification does not require anyone to stop exploring the respective bilateral connections of discourse with other modes of action, production, and signification. Those connections can assist us in placing discourse—any discourse—in a number of illuminating contexts. For example, we may wish to study discourse as doing, compare its motives and effects with those of other strategies and tactics, and stress its ethical or polit-

8. Cf., for instance, Ake W. Edfeldt, *Silent Speech and Silent Reading* (Chicago: University of Chicago Press, 1960), on the physiological and Garrett Stewart, *Reading Voices: Literature and Phonotext* (Berkeley and Los Angeles: University of California Press, 1990), on the semiotic and aesthetic implications of what Stewart calls "phonemic reading." See also the following passage from Eudora Welty's autobiographical work, *One Writer's Beginnings* (Cambridge: Harvard University Press, 1983), pp. 12–13: "Ever since I was first read to, then started reading to myself, there has never been a line that I didn't *hear*. As my eyes followed the sentence, a voice was saying it silently to me. It isn't my mother's voice, or the voice of any person I can identify, certainly not my own. . . . It is to me the voice of the story or the poem itself. . . . My own words, when I am at work on a story, I hear too as they go, in the same voice that I hear when I read in books." Concerning nonverbal thinking (by deaf-mute persons, for example) see note 29 below.

9. See Karl Popper, *Objective Knowledge* (Oxford: Clarendon, 1972), p. 106, where a "third world" of the "*objective contents of thought,* especially of scientific and poetic thoughts and of works of art" is distinguished from the "first" and "second" worlds of physical and of mental states. A sympathetic, albeit critical, commentary on Popper's pertinent ideas can be found in Jürgen Habermas, *The Theory of Communicative Action* (note 2 to Prologue), 1: 76–84. For a more radical theory of both scientific and artistic worldmaking, see Nelson Goodman, *Ways of Worldmaking* (note 4 to Prologue).

ical aspects as if all verbal practice were mainly action or interaction. Or we may wish to study discourse as making, compare its methods and products with those of other arts and technologies, and stress its aesthetic or economic aspects as if all verbal practice were mainly creation or production. Finally, we may wish to study discourse as meaning, compare its codes and messages with those of other ways of storing and conveying information, and stress its semiotic or hermeneutic aspects as if all verbal practice were mainly signification or significance. Yes, we may. But it is wise not to reduce any particular discourse to "nothing but" action, production, or signification, because such reduction mystifies—without diminishing—the pull exerted by every utterance, text, and thought in two other directions as well.

*Speaking, Writing, Thinking*

The twentieth century has witnessed the advent of technology that permits both the unwritten storage of speech and, to some extent, the external, nonverbal monitoring of unspoken thought (for example, dreams). Yet speech has remained our chief means of instantaneously exchanging quasi-verbal thoughts, and writing (including typing, typesetting, and other modes of text production) has so far remained our most common means of perpetuating both speech and thought. Thought will probably continue as the only means of internalizing whatever messages are signified by speech and writing, as well as by such machines as tape recorders, lie detectors, electroencephalographs, and computers. Signification and significance therefore have a special relation to thought, and the question that readily arises is, Whose thought?

The user of a lie detector or a computer does not construe meaning by reconstructing what those machines "mean" in the sense of *vouloir dire*—the French expression for both "mean" and (more literally) "want to say." The operator of such machines knows that they provide essentially preprogrammed answers to queries submitted to them. It is important to realize that our initial response to a text we read or to an utterance we hear is frequently similar to the response of a person operating a lie detector or a computer: we construe the text or utterance according to the questions we expect it to answer. For this reason, it has even been argued that the listener and especially the reader (rather than the speaker or the usually absent writer) determine the operative meaning of discourse.[10]

We can never be sure, of course, that a listener's or reader's private, subjective meaning is equivalent to what the speaker or writer meant; we often discover that it is not. Nonetheless, the intersubjective dimension of discourse as action within the shared lifeworld of speakers and listeners makes the possible gap between their respective meanings principally bridgeable and, in most instances of consequential verbal practice, negligible.[11] We learn the typical range of a word's meaning, as well as the general grammatical rules for combining words into sentences, from our interaction with other human beings. Even the specific communicative purpose of a particular utterance and the shade of meaning intended or involuntarily revealed by a

10. Well before recent reader-response critics explicitly claimed the right of individual readers or interpretive communities to trespass on authorial property, two representative New Critics had argued that the poem "is detached from the author at birth" and "belongs to the public": see W. K. Wimsatt and Monroe C. Beardsley, "The Intentional Fallacy" (1946), in W. K. Wimsatt, *The Verbal Icon* (Lexington: University of Kentucky Press, 1954).

11. For the intersubjective basis of subjective meaning, see Alfred Schutz, *The Phenomenology of the Social World*, trans. George Walsh and Frederick Lehnert (Evanston, Ill.: Northwestern University Press, 1967). In his later works Schutz made influential use of Edmund Husserl's term *Lebenswelt* ("lifeworld" or "world of daily life"), which I employ in Schutz's sense; see Aron Gurwitsch's introduction to Alfred Schutz, *Studies in Phenomenological Philosophy*, ed. Ilse Schutz (The Hague: Nijhoff, 1966), pp. xi–xxxi. This is vol. 1 of his *Collected Papers*, 3 vols. (1962–66). Husserl's use of the term is placed in the context of the intellectual history of the last hundred years by Hans Ulrich Gumbrecht, "*Everyday-World* and *Life-World* as Philosophical Concepts: A Genealogical Approach," *New Literary History* 24 (1993): 745–61.

certain speaker in a particular situation are far from being private: they are embedded in the shared public lifeworld of listeners and speakers.[12] A large part of the meaning of utterances is thus eminently intersubjective, and listeners typically manage to progress rather quickly from the initial construction of a meaning they themselves would have expressed by the spoken words toward a reconstruction of the meaning the speaker most probably intended.

Much greater is the difficulty readers face in trying to understand what a writer (who may be distant, dead, or anonymous) meant or involuntarily revealed. As we are told in a famous passage of Plato's *Phaedrus* (275), the absent "parent" of a piece of writing cannot protect such an abandoned offspring from interpretive abuse, while the text (unlike a living interlocutor) is unable to defend itself. It is clear that some texts—especially some religious, legal, and literary texts—have so endeared themselves to many readers that the history of their interpretation resembles an unending series of custody battles among aspiring foster parents. To avoid the charge of hermeneutic child abuse, readers must observe the rules of textual conduct accepted in their interpretive communities. But within each of these communities and across the dividing lines between them, interpreters who have managed to silence certain aspects of an adopted text ought to engage in open dialogue with other interpreters who can speak for those aspects. Indeed, one crucial function of recent feminist and ethnic critics has been to lend voice to heretofore silenced meanings in favored, as well as neglected, texts.

Just as debates reflecting a text's impact on current readers keep us alert to its power as a thing done, the text's continued ap-

---

12. See Mikhail Bakhtin, "The Problem of Speech Genres," in "*Speech Genres*" *and Other Late Essays,* trans. Vern W. McGee, ed. Caryl Emerson and Michael Holquist (Austin: University of Texas Press, 1986), p. 91: "Each utterance is filled with echoes and reverberations of other utterances to which it is related. . . . Each utterance refutes, affirms, supplements, and relies on others, presupposes them to be known, and somehow takes them into account."

peal over time demonstrates its efficacy as a thing made.[13] Since writing results in lasting physical objects—say, black marks on white paper—it enables discourse to remain effective beyond the scene of its initial occurrence. Just like its more vocal and much younger cousin, the acoustic recording of speech, writing can transfer the "force" and "effect" of discourse into ever new spatial, temporal, and semiotic environments.[14] Such transferral typically liberates the impact of the verbally made (and by extension the impact of the verbal maker) from the original intersubjective context of a particular fleeting moment. In principle one could even argue that the objective context of anything written is everything written. The effective context of a particular text while the text is being understood by a particular reader is, of course, much more specific and far less textual than that: it is a fusion of the relevant segments of the reader's and the text's respective horizons. That is to say, textual understanding brings about a fusion of as much of the reader's intersubjective lifeworld and as much of the text's intertextual context as become subjectively mobilized in a

13. The history of literary reception shows that different readers will "concretize" the same text in many ways in the course of its "life." Texts will thus be included or not included in the canon of a particular tradition for many different reasons. Conversely, the history of texts as transactions (things done to and by interpreting readers) is closely tied to their history as verbal objects (things made and preserved for future interpretive transactions). For the reader's need and power to "concretize" texts in an individual way, see chapter 13, "The 'Life' of a Literary Work," in Roman Ingarden, *The Literary Work of Art: An Investigation on the Borderlines of Ontology, Logic, and Theory of Literature* (1931; 3d German ed. 1965), trans. George G. Grabowicz (Evanston, Ill.: Northwestern University Press, 1973), pp. 331–55.

14. Following J. L. Austin (note 1 above), philosophers, linguists, and literary critics have for some time been exploring the *il*locutionary force of what we do *in* saying something and the *per*locutionary effect of what we do *by* saying something. As the controversy between Jacques Derrida and John Searle demonstrates, Austin's revival of the ancient rhetorical insight that we *do* things with words can elicit almost disparate interpretations. It is well known, for example, that Derrida (unlike Austin and Searle) considers writing rather than speech the paradigmatic discursive activity. See esp. Jacques Derrida, "Signature Event Context," *Glyph* 1 (1977): 172–97, and "Limited inc abc," *Glyph* 2 (1977): 162–254, as well as John Searle, "Reiterating the Differences: A Reply to Derrida," *Glyph* 1 (1977): 198–208.

particular reading experience.[15] For example, if an American college student of the 1990s has not read any Milton and has not heard of potential conflicts between ethics and technology, his or her understanding of Mary Shelley's *Frankenstein* will not be influenced by *Paradise Lost* or by the recent debates about human gene splicing.

Subjective, objective, and intersubjective features are intertwined in our most private thoughts as well. After all, the thoughts occurring to "subjective" individuals occur in the "objective" domain of brains and typically internalize remembered or imagined verbal interactions that a person had, might have had, or plans to have with other people. To be sure, when we associate mental events with discourse, we tend to regard them as a particular mind's own silent speech or invisible writing.[16] Since, however, a great deal of quasi-verbal thought is based on remembered words spoken or written by others, the meaning of much of what I quasi-verbally think is mine only to the extent that I have appropriated it from the intersubjective "conversation of mankind."[17]

15. As the borrowed phrase "fusion of horizons" indicates, I wish to correlate the poststructuralist notion of all-encompassing intertextuality with the phenomenological notion of all-encompassing lifeworld along the lines suggested by Hans-Georg Gadamer, *Truth and Method* (1960; 5th German ed. 1986), 2d revised English ed., translation revised by Joel Weinsheimer and Donald G. Marshall (New York: Crossroad, 1989), pp. 300–307 et passim. But I also think that Gadamer's concept of a presumably unified tradition fails to allow for significant differences among the respective hermeneutic situations of different, albeit contemporary, readers.

16. For example, the founding father of behavioristic psychology insisted that "'thinking' is largely *subvocal talking*." The founding father of psychoanalysis in turn suggested that all perceptions (and presumably other mental processes too) permanently inscribe themselves on something like a "mystic writing pad" below the erasable surface of consciousness. See John B. Watson, *Behaviorism* (1924), 3d ed. (New York: Norton, 1970), p. 268, and Sigmund Freud, "A Note upon the 'Mystic Writing-Pad'" (1925), in *The Standard Edition of the Complete Psychological Works of Sigmund Freud*, ed. James Strachey, 24 vols. (London: Hogarth, 1953–74), 19 (1964): 225–32.

17. The quoted phrase is borrowed from the title of Michael Oakeshott, *The Voice of Poetry in the Conversation of Mankind* (London: Bowes, 1959).

Now, if we take the notion of internalized conversation or interior dialogue seriously, we should conceive of the thinking person not only as silently speaking but also as inwardly listening to the silent messages that come to each of us, in part at least, through the internalized voices of other human beings. For some purposes, however, the analogy of reading may serve better than that of listening: it evokes the hermeneutic effort required for deciphering what nature, culture, and our own identity are "trying to say" but can actually "mean" only as we engage in the internal acts of reading our minds. On this view—whose analogical function it is prudent to remember—nature, culture, and even our selves are no more fully present to us than a text can be.[18] Whatever occurs to me (in both the external and the mental senses of "occur") awaits transformation, through a kind of internal reading, into meaningful messages. The messages may originate from what they make intelligible as the physical or the social world; or, like dreams attributed to inarticulate fears or repressed desires, they may be assumed to come from personal feelings not yet or no longer lingual. But the very transformation of the readable into the read affects the transforming consciousness itself. Having assimilated new meanings to my thereby transformed self, "I" now have the challenge of reading a new "me"—of becoming more fully conscious of what my self has just become.[19]

18. See "Some Consequences of Four Incapacities," in *Collected Papers of Charles Sanders Peirce*, 8 vols. (1931–58), vol. 5, *Pragmatism and Pragmaticism*, ed. Charles Hartshorne and Paul Weiss (Cambridge: Harvard University Press, 1934), esp. pp. 188–89, on human beings as "external signs" to themselves: "Since man can think only by means of words or other external symbols, these might turn round and say: 'You mean nothing that we have not taught you, and then only so far as you address some word as the interpretant of your thought.' In fact, therefore, men and words reciprocally educate each other, each increase of a man's information involves and is involved by, a corresponding increase of a word's information. . . . The word or sign which man uses *is* the man himself."

19. G. H. Mead's different juxtaposition of "I" and "me" is discussed below in chapter 4. Mead characterizes the "me," to which his "I" responds, as the socially constructed dimension of the self. My temporal distinction here between "I" and "me" in turn stresses that each human consciousness continually pulls itself up by its own bootstraps through an unfinishable process of self-decoding.

Unfortunately, the notion of thinking as silently reading from an internal writing pad tends to suggest the existence of a homuncular superconsciousness observing from the outside, as it were, our spontaneous "stream of thought" (William James) or "psychical primary process" (Sigmund Freud).[20] Such a view might impel those who hold it less cautiously than James or Freud to imagine the existence of another, and then yet another, homunculus reading the mind of the mind's first or second reader—deciphering the first or second mental decipherer—and so on ad infinitum. It is clearly preferable to shift the heuristic metaphor from a single monitored flux or process to an exchange of information as it exists, for instance, in a network of several interlinked computer monitors and keyboards. The ever ongoing internal communication implied by this image of multiple selfhood is not interpretive regress but quasi-conversational progress. In other words, the interactive view of the mind as network does not make us worry about who interprets the last interpreter. Rather, it makes us wonder who will respond next in the lively dialogue between, among, and within the multiple selves that each of us jointly is.[21]

Beyond doubt, widespread literacy has helped establish the modern sense of unified yet variegated personal identity. The ability to write and read permits us to preserve and reexperience

20. See chapter 9, "The Stream of Thought," in William James, *The Principles of Psychology* (note 3 to Prologue), 1:224–90. Freud's contrast between primary and secondary processes first appears in his posthumously published "Project for a Scientific Psychology" (1895); in *Standard Edition* (note 16 above), 1:324–27 et passim.

21. I find the following description of mental polyphony very illuminating: "Any creature (including ourselves) consists of a set of linked yet quasi-autonomous modules. Each of us is, as it were, a delegation but there is only one microphone." See Derek Bickerton, *Language and Species* (Chicago: University of Chicago Press, 1990), pp. 218–19. In my view the "microphone" changes hands frequently even without the impact of "greater than normal" stimuli. While in possession of the microphone, each "speaker"—the temporary center of quasi-verbal awareness—can offer a running commentary on the unruly "proceedings" of the delegate assembly in which that commentator nonetheless continues to participate. Small wonder we get confused sometimes: each commentary covers from a different vantage point the multiple self's progress along the social, natural, and personal fault lines of culture, existence, and experience.

otherwise fleeting thoughts and utterances. Photographs or videotapes—products of an essentially postliterate technology—do not really show us who we are but serve as reified reminders of how we were.[22] By contrast, when I am reading something that I know I wrote some time ago, I am impelled to reappropriate textual meaning that is at once alien ("out there" in the objective and intersubjective world) and very much my own.[23] A reflective reading of my own writing thus reconnects my public person with the private. It also enables me to experience existential continuity between different temporal phases of an evolving self—*I* am at any moment what my *me* has just become—in the deeply historical sense of ever identical, yet ever changing, selfhood.

Writing and printing contribute a great deal to the material and cultural well-being of literate societies. But the superabundance of printed documents in our typographic (and increasingly computerized) culture has an alienating effect as well. Medical and credit reports, for example, establish what counts as the official state of our health and wealth. By determining the kind of insurance coverage and bank loans we can henceforth obtain, such reports often serve as society's self-fulfilling prophecies about the

22. In "Rhetoric of the Image," in *The Responsibility of Forms*, trans. Richard Howard (New York: Hill, 1985), pp. 21–40, Roland Barthes attributes only to photography "the always stupefying evidence of *this is how it was.*" For him "the cinema is not an animated photograph; in it, the *having-been-there* vanishes, giving way to a *being-there* of the thing; this would explain how there can be a history of the cinema, without a real break with the previous arts of fiction" (pp. 33–34). As the last phrase suggests, Barthes's supposed contrast between photographs and films in fact articulates a contrast between two modes of reading images: the documentary and the fictional. It seems to me that viewers of their own past images can hardly avoid approaching those images, whether still or in motion, in the documentary mode. For example, an elderly performer watching his or her filmed enactment of a youthful role is likely to perceive a "having been there," whereas the fictional character—say, Hamlet or Ophelia—will strike other viewers of the movie screen (or even of a stage photograph) as "being there."

23. Such reappropriation de-reifies, so to speak, the written text's initial reification of my personal identity. Writing's potential for alienating reification is the seamy side of what Godzich and Kittay appreciate as its potential for fostering self-referential autonomy. See Wlad Godzich and Jeffrey Kittay, *The Emergence of Prose: An Essay in Prosaics* (Minneapolis: University of Minnesota Press, 1987), p. 209 et passim.

length and quality of our lives. As latter-day oracles, some damaging documents may in fact presage the uninsurable or homeless future of entire families as well.

The widespread circulation of printed matter no doubt affects the illiterate members of a modern society in a particularly adverse fashion.[24] While the unlettered and functionally illiterate in a postoral civilization receive only a portion of the benefits that literacy confers on competent writers and readers, they are especially exposed to the objectifying impact that printed documents tend to have on human beings. Take a passport, a green card, or a driver's license: each identifies its holder from without much as a posted sign in a museum or a zoo identifies rocks or animals. As long as some men and women cannot even decipher, let alone attempt to interpret, the writings whereby their society defines them, their documented identities must remain essentially foreign to both the public and the private conduct of their lives. Such externally imposed identity will not help diversify the intersubjective roles that the literate and the illiterate alike perform within their unequally shared lifeworld of social interactions. Nor will it facilitate the subjective glimpses that every human organism continually struggles to catch of its own evolving selfhood. Indeed, the way a literate bureaucracy can impose on the unlettered the pseudo-objective identity of printed documents almost recalls the lethal role assigned to a particularly violent form of writing in Franz Kafka's "Penal Colony."

## Communication, Expression, Representation

Language may have acquired its privileged place in the human lifeworld because it is an equally suitable vehicle for three major semiotic functions: expression, communication, and representa-

24. The deprivative orality of illiterate people in an alphabetic civilization is very different from the thriving "primary" orality of a culture "untouched by writing." See Walter Ong, *Orality and Literacy: The Technologizing of the Word* (London: Methuen, 1982), pp. 11, 31 et passim on "primary oral cultures."

tion.[25] Indeed, those functions manifest themselves in the very structure of all known languages as the first, the second, and the third grammatical person: I *express myself* as I *communicate* with *you* in discourse that can *represent them*.[26] To be sure, the representational, communicative, and expressive functions of signification find rudimentary analogues quite far down the evolutionary ladder. For example, the sensory apparatus of animals obviously represents certain aspects of their environment; their threatening, warning, and mating signals have communicative functions; and their leaving behind odors, footprints, excrement, and offspring inscribes into their surrounds traces of involuntary self-expression. By means of human or protohuman language, however, our prehistoric ancestors managed to advance from isolated sensory impressions to conceptually structured and shareable representations of a world; from one-directional signals emitted to repulse, alert, or attract others to sustained reciprocal communication; and from making a mark on the environment to producing artifacts expressive of conscious design. In other words, *Homo loquens* had to emerge along with *Homo sapiens*, *Homo politicus*, and *Homo faber* if meaning, doing, and making—mental representation, face-to-face communication, and material self-expression— were to complete their respective transitions from signification to significance, from reaction to interaction, from mostly instinctual

25. See Karl Bühler's account of the "linguistic sign" (*Sprachzeichen*) as expression by sender, as appeal to receiver, and as representation of objects and states of affairs in *Sprachtheorie* (Jena: Fischer, 1934), pp. 24–33, English version *Theory of Language*, trans. Donald Fraser Goodwin (Amsterdam: Benjamins, 1990), pp. 30–39.

26. Much more will be said about pronominal perspectives in chapter 3. But two qualifications as to the respective parallels between expression, communication, and representation on the one hand and the first, second, and third grammatical person on the other should be noted right away. (1) I can *indirectly* communicate with unaddressed third persons when I assume that they will read or that they are eavesdropping on what I am telling you about them. (2) Through explicit pronominal reference, I can *temporarily* add to my always implied role as first-person sender and to your always implied role as second-person receiver of a verbal message the additional role, always assigned to all third persons, of being spoken or written about.

22

excretion and reproduction to fully intelligent production and creation.[27]

In his *Philosophical Investigations* Ludwig Wittgenstein famously asked: "What is left over if I subtract the fact that my arm goes up from the fact that I raise my arm?"[28] In a similar vein, I have often wondered: What is left over if I subtract the fact that words are uttered or inscribed from the fact that I speak or write? It seems to me that the residue in question is mental representation—an act of meaning that I perform and expect my listeners or readers to replicate or at least approximate. Without such replication or approximation no intersubjective communication is achieved even if both verbal expression (the objectifying of the sender's thoughts in discourse) and quasi-verbal representation (the subjectifying of discourse in a receiver's thoughts) have occurred.

To be sure, acts of meaning need not be accompanied by acts of speaking, writing, listening, or reading. But even if we "subtract" the external acts of uttering or inscribing, our acts of meaning remain quasi-verbal building blocks of mental discourse.[29] Furthermore, the quasi-verbal acts of meaning that make up "the un-

27. See Raymond Tallis, *The Explicit Animal: A Defence of Human Consciousness* (Basingstoke: Macmillan, 1991), p. 230: "Language is not, of course, the only medium in which reflexive self-consciousness can unfold; but it is a matrix in which higher-order unfoldings most typically take place; in which, for example, I become most elaborately aware of your awareness of my awareness of me."

28. Section 621 in Ludwig Wittgenstein, *Philosophical Investigations*, trans. G. E. M. Anscombe, 3d ed. (New York: Macmillan, 1968), p. 161.

29. Whereas the different parts of a brain communicate with each other in the language of electric charges and chemical valences, the various "parts" of a mind seem to understand each other best when they silently converse, as it were, in a human language. But such an internal dialogue should not be conceived according to the exclusive paradigm of oral communication. Since most of us primarily communicate by pronouncing sounds, it is easy to forget that deaf-mute users of a sign language think in terms of its nonverbal vocabulary and syntax while the hand and arm muscles they would employ for the visible production of signs in intersubjective communication become—at least subliminally—activated. For a telling anecdote, see Oliver Sacks, *Seeing Voices: A Journey into the World of the Deaf* (Berkeley and Los Angeles: University of California Press, 1989), p. 35. Even hearing people often convey meaning without uttering audible words, and in our age of laptop computers and electronic mail, mental representation is likely to continue its historical trend of being increasingly

uttered conversation of the soul with herself" not only are quasi-*locutionary*, they are (to invoke two more terms from Austin's theory of speech acts) quasi-*illocutionary* and quasi-*perlocutionary* as well.[30] I can, for example, threaten myself with lung cancer (should I fail to quit smoking) or promise myself a nice cup of tea (should I finish drafting this paragraph before 4:30 P.M.). As long as I am fully engaged in the interpretive articulation of what goes on in my own mind, such a silent, self-addressed threat or promise carries the same kind of "illocutionary force" as attaches to actually pronounced or inscribed threats and promises. Even "perlocutionary effect"—my becoming convinced about the connection between cancer and smoking or my expecting to be rewarded for efficient progress in composition—can occur without any words being spoken or written. Thus the view that our thinking echoes, accompanies, or prepares *grammatically* structured

aligned with written expression rather than oral communication. A philosopher friend, for instance, tells me that he tends to think with his fingers. Not being a proficient typist, I have never caught myself doing that, but I recognize that the degree of association between oral speech and mentation differs widely depending on the individuals, cultures, and referential domains involved. For example, I seldom think my chess thoughts with the names of the pieces in mind. Nor do my musical or chess thoughts seem to be couched in English, German, or Hungarian—the languages in which I quasi-verbally think about most other matters, including the question whether my musical or chess thoughts are quasi-verbal.

30. The quoted phrase occurs in Jowett's translation of Plato's *Sophist* (263; see note 5 above). For J. L. Austin's concepts of locutionary, illocutionary, and perlocutionary acts—what we do *as* we say something, *in* saying something, and *by* saying something—see note 1 above, esp. p. 121: "The locutionary act . . . has a *meaning*; the illocutionary act . . . has a certain *force* in saying something; the perlocutionary act . . . is the *achieving of* certain *effects* by saying something" (Austin's italics). In "Literary Theory: A Compass for Critics," *Critical Inquiry* 3 (1976): 369–86, I relate speech acts to their nonverbal context by distinguishing (1) *pre*locutionary motivation from *per*locutionary intention and (2) *post*locutionary outcome from *per*locutionary impact (see esp. p. 376 n. 13). In terms of this book, the following set of examples may be helpful. I feel cold (objective prelocutionary motivation), want to make you close the window (subjective perlocutionary intention), and request or command that you do so (intersubjective illocutionary force); you recognize the force of the request or command (intersubjective illocutionary uptake), decide to comply (subjective perlocutionary impact), and actually close the window (objective postlocutionary outcome).

sentences deserves to be supplemented by the view that our minds both engage in and respond to the *rhetoric* of quasi-speech acts when we inwardly talk and listen to ourselves. To the extent that my mentation goes beyond rehearsing what I have been told or what I expect to be saying, it allows me to fathom—mentally represent—instances of as yet nonverbal meaning whose entry into objectifying expression and intersubjective communication has to await riper historical circumstances. For example, the desire for flying must have been mentally represented (in preverbal feelings and quasi-verbal thoughts) for a long time before it was first communicated (say, in some analogue of the Icarus legend) and eventually realized (through such lasting material expressions of human ingenuity as hot-air balloons and airplanes). The desire for cosmic and social justice is an equally imaginative impulse of human mentation and has by now been variously communicated (for instance, in the Book of Job and the Declaration of Independence) but still awaits more tangible expression through higher degrees of material equality, communal fraternity, and personal liberty than are generally available today.[31]

Thanks to the rhetorical power of desire and the creative imagination, the meaning mind tends to initiate the processes whereby things get done and made in human worlds. Yet kings and presidents hardly stand lower on the social ladder than court philosophers and latter-day political thinkers. Nor do brainy inventors typically outrank (or outearn) our "captains of industry." Even if poets and other visionaries are, as Percy Shelley believed, the "unacknowledged legislators of the world," they are rather slow in getting their bills enacted, let alone enforced.[32] Indeed,

31. Although the possibility of flying could easily suggest itself to humans through their observation of birds and insects, our age-old yearning for cosmic and social justice must have originated in a complex set of self-assertive and self-transcending motives.

32. See "A Defence of Poetry" (1821), in *The Complete Works of Percy Bysshe Shelley*, ed. Roger Ingpen and Walker E. Peck, 10 vols. (1927; rpt. New York: Gordian Press, 1965), 7:140.

powerful political and military "doers" often tell their subordinate advisers what to mean, just as they tell their laborers what to make. In the political arena especially, spoken communication continues to carry more outward prestige than mental representation or textual expression. Substantially aided by the ideas and rhetorical devices of unacknowledged speechwriters, men and women of power tend to appeal to the public as speakers rather than as thinkers or writers. Our postliterate politicians in particular like to maintain the fiction of improvised speaking while their teleprompters remain invisible to the television audience.

Behind the scenes, of course, modern bureaucratic governments mainly conduct their business by way of written (including typed or keypunched) expression. This is partly why the authority of the written and the need to interpret it both in speech and in further writing have gradually grown in most literate societies. The increasing availability of printed texts in the five centuries of our Gutenberg era especially contributed to the shifting of general interest, noted by Hans-Georg Gadamer among other scholars, "from the speaking and writing of speeches to the understanding of the written and to the interpreting of it."[33] Much legal debate, both among legislators and among the voters electing them, centers today on the constitutionality of laws and the desirability of constitutional amendments. Most such debate aims at legitimizing, modifying, or dismissing the power vested › in one set of written expressions by means of another set of subsequently produced documents.

The commercial world of inventories, contracts, bookkeeping, and statistics also relies on printed or even computerized words, numbers, and graphics. There is a significant parallel between the extramental storing of information and the extracorporeal accumulation of capital—in other words, between communication and labor in their respective states of suspended animation.

33. "The Hermeneutics of Suspicion," in *Hermeneutics: Questions and Projects,* ed. Gary Shapiro and Alan Sica (Amherst: University of Massachusetts Press, 1984), p. 55.

Small wonder that Plato's objections to the written word's depersonalizing impact on human meaning are echoed by later Marxist objections to the depersonalizing effect of accumulated capital on human doing.[34] The two kinds of feared domination of the living present by a fossilized past have more in common than seems generally recognized. After all, a literate tradition's accumulation of what might be called cultural capital alienates work from author no less radically (and perhaps even more insidiously) than the private or public owner's accumulation of wealth can alienate the power and product of labor from slave, serf, or other worker.[35]

That authors of texts often get honorable mention for their ideas expressed in writing should be small comfort to any would-be communicator familiar with the motley history of often willful reception of even the most celebrated classics. Having "died into" their texts,[36] authors can no more influence the future use made of their works than the industrial makers of tools or weapons can influence the future use made of the fruits of their labor. The dehumanizing effects of both kinds of alienation can diminish only if authors and laborers manage to regard their readers and employers as partners in signification or production rather than (as readers and employers too often are) self-serving exploiters of

34. Cf. Plato, *Phaedrus* 274–78, and "Seventh Letter" 342–44, as well as Karl Marx and Friedrich Engels, *Manifesto of the Communist Party*, in *Collected Works* (New York: International, 1975–92), 6 (1976): 499. The authorship of Plato's fascinating "Seventh Letter" is widely disputed. Hans-Georg Gadamer, "Dialectic and Sophism in Plato's *Seventh Letter*" (1964), in *Dialogue and Dialectic: Eight Hermeneutical Studies on Plato*, trans. P. Christopher Smith (New Haven: Yale University Press, 1980), considers the text authentic; Ludwig Edelstein, *Plato's Seventh Letter* (Leiden: Brill, 1966), comes to the opposite conclusion; Walter Bröcker, "Der philosophische Exkurs in Platons siebentem Brief," *Hermes* 91 (1963): 416–25, proposed an interesting compromise.

35. Pierre Bourdieu's use of the term "cultural capital" is different; see esp. his *Distinction: A Social Critique of the Judgement of Taste*, trans. Richard Nice (Cambridge: Harvard University Press, 1984) pp. 80–83 et passim.

36. Roland Barthes speaks of "The Death of the Author" in a related sense; see his *Image—Music—Text*, selected and trans. Stephen Heath (New York: Hill and Wang, 1977), pp. 142–48.

other people's textual or material efforts. This is a rather tall order for authors and laborers alike, as well as for other people needing to be paid and wanting to be appreciated for whatever they do, make, or mean. But the order can be filled to some degree in nurturing cultural climates of responsive textual reception and responsible social governance.

Unfortunately, personal alienation may not be the worst danger facing humanity today. We are eager and able to do, make, and mean a lot more than other species, and the accelerating tempo of our lives has lately made us deplete and pollute the environment much faster than it can be replenished and cleansed by the earth's natural rhythms. It remains to be seen whether our combustion and nuclear technologies, buttressed by electronic means of communication, expression, and representation, will bring about unprecedented natural disasters or will help us avert them.

## Intersubjective, Objective, Subjective

In the preceding sections I suggest that all discourse involves action, production, and signification, and that doing, making, and meaning tend respectively to predominate in speaking, writing, and thinking—the prime vehicles of communication, expression, and representation in our culture. In discussing those three triads I occasionally invoke a fourth—intersubjective, objective, and subjective—whose relation to the others is explored further in the next several pages.[37]

37. A lucid discussion of the "opposition between subjective and objective points of view" can be found in Thomas Nagel, *Mortal Questions* (Cambridge: Cambridge University Press, 1979), pp. 196–213. Unfortunately, Nagel tends to conflate what I think are aspects of the intersubjective with one or the other of his two categories. By contrast, several contributions to the just-published volume *Rethinking Objectivity*, ed. Allan Megill (Durham, N.C.: Duke University Press, 1994), shed light on the intersubjective construal of much that often counts as objective or subjective. My own concepts of the subjective, objective,

The terms "subjective" and "objective" usually imply a distinct cleavage in the universe between Descartes's *res cogitans* and *res extensa*—between consciousness and the material world. This dualistic view of "things" (*res*) as either "thinking" or spatially "extended" has long been under attack by monistic materialists and monistic idealists alike. In the context of the present study, the rejection of Cartesian dualism by a third kind of monism deserves particular attention. I have in mind a line of thought that goes back at least to Marx and can lead to a firm belief in what Peter L. Berger and Thomas Luckmann termed "the social construction of reality."[38]

It is hard to quarrel with the view that each of us is "socialized" from early childhood into seeing the world (including ourselves) as the practices and institutions of our culture make us see it. But if consistently held, this view entails the troublesome corollary that even the desire of nonconformists and revolutionaries for deviation or innovation stems from the social framework they are bent on subverting. In particular, a nonconformist or revolutionary appeal to objective nature or to subjective freedom must be ruled out of court if it is only society that can give us the idea that our intersubjective relations should be freer or more natural than they are. Besides, even the most "free" and "natural" society of the past or the future would, on such a view, have to be intersubjectively constructing what its deluded members mistake for their objective or subjective, natural or liberated reality.

---

and intersubjective as complementary modes of being toward, of, and with the world are analogous to the subjective, objective, and social "world relations" distinguished by Jürgen Habermas and to Rom Harré's concepts of personal, physical, and social being. But in many details, as well as in certain basic assumptions, my triad functions quite differently from theirs (see note 2 to Prologue).

38. See note 1 to Prologue. Berger and Luckmann's influential book has, or should have, introduced American sociologists to much Continental (mostly German) thought within and around *Wissenssoziologie*—the sociology of knowledge.

The shrewder proponents of the view that all reality is socially constructed do acknowledge that their own view and the reality presupposed by it must themselves be socially constructed. Their position thus becomes structurally similar to so-called solipsism—the solitary self's claim that all contents of its consciousness are imaginary because, *solus ipse*, it alone exists. Neither position can be substantiated or, for that matter, defeated from without because each denies, precisely, that there is anything outside its own purview. Why, then, is it more customary to reject solipsism, which considers subjectivity an absolute, than it is to reject the view that reality is socially constructed—a position that amounts to making intersubjectivity an absolute? The answer, or a good part of it, lies in the media of discourse we must use to communicate with one another. Although you and I, in our separate private thoughts, may well embrace solipsism, we cannot publicly share a solipsistic view in speech or writing—who would exclusively exist, you or I? Conversely, of course, it is much easier to talk or write about the biological predetermination or social construction of individual selves than to be completely and sincerely persuaded by such a thesis in the privacy of one's own mind.

Now, it would be odd to settle for a pair of mutually damaging confirmations: the confirmation in private, mental discourse of the prime existence of one's self and the confirmation in public speech or writing of the prime existence of societies. Moreover, a rigid distinction between private and public vehicles of discourse is quite unjustified. After all, "public" conversation and "private" thinking often occur simultaneously and, in any case, each exerts a constitutive impact on the other. The following assumption therefore seems sufficiently warranted: Both experience and culture—subjective selves and intersubjective societies—exist, yet each of those dimensions of being human owes its existence to the other as the two emerge and develop in constant interplay.

But how does objectivity come into the picture of verbal practice that I have just outlined? We can no doubt think, talk, and write about ourselves and others *as if* neither we nor they were objectively existing human beings. Some who deny objective existence embrace a psychocentric view deserving the paradoxical name of pluralistic solipsism. They hold that only subjective selves truly exist and that each such self projects, from within itself, a world including other selves that appear real to it.[39] Other refusers of objectivity take a sociocentric stance. According to fairly new but influential versions of this orientation, only intersubjective discourse truly exists, and it projects from within itself various speaker or author functions, listener or reader positions, fiction or reality effects.[40] Remarkably, however, radical subjectivists and radical intersubjectivists alike produce texts, which means that their own mental representations and oral communications occasionally turn into quite palpable written expression. Since most texts outlast the personal and social circumstances of their initial production, they afford readers access to the objective domain of things made. By calling it objective, I don't mean to imply that this domain is stable or stagnant. Always in the making, the domain of products—whether natural or cultural—is in fact a dynamic force field of cosmic and human productivity.

Let me put it this way. The Cartesian "I think, therefore I am" requires a "social" supplement: "we talk and listen, therefore you too are." But these axioms of personal and social being also require a "natural" supplement: "Writing and reading occur, there-

39. The more philosophically inclined among the "solipsistic pluralists" may seek (and occasionally find) support for their worldview in the work of such idealist thinkers as Berkeley, Leibniz, and Fichte.

40. Resolutely "sociocentric" considerations of discourse include the following: Michel Foucault, "What Is an Author?" in his *Language, Countermemory, Practice: Selected Essays and Interviews*, ed. Donald F. Bouchard, trans. Donald F. Bouchard and Sherry Simon (Ithaca: Cornell University Press, 1977), esp. pp. 124–31 on institutional author functions; Roland Barthes, *S/Z*, trans. Richard Miller (New York: Hill, 1974), p. 10 on apparently subjective yet stereotypically precoded readers; Etienne Balibar and Pierre Macherey, "On Literature as an Ideological Form: Some Marxist Propositions," in *Untying the Text: A Post-structuralist Reader*, ed. Robert Young (London: Routledge, 1981), esp. pp. 89–93 on ideologically produced—"hallucinatory"—reality effects and fiction effects.

fore the world is." The first conclusion stems from experienced meaning as the mainly private, subjective dimension of discourse. The second conclusion stems from the cultural doing involved in the oral acts of speech that exemplify the relatively social, intersubjective dimension of discourse. The connection between the third conclusion and existential making—the production and reproduction of durable texts as the mainly transpersonal, objective dimension of discourse—may be less evident. But it is forcefully suggested by the time-honored metaphor identifying the material products of cosmic creativity as parts of a decipherable text—the so-called "book of nature."

I hardly need point out that two equally familiar topoi express the first two conclusions in metaphoric terms. "Life is a dream" (or might as well be a dream) if one's sole source of cognitive certainty resides in the private *cogito*; and "the world is a stage" indeed if all reality is constructed by players of socially scripted roles. The book of nature; the dream of life; the stage of the world: there is an extensive literature[41] on each of the age-old topoi that I here associate with the objective, the subjective, and the intersubjective dimensions of being human. In the not too distant future I also plan to explore what the metaphoric trio suggests concerning the fictional aspects of human worlds and the existential, experiential, and cultural aspects of fiction.

How did human beings come to develop a threefold attitude toward themselves as organisms, as players of roles, and as self-conscious centers of personal awareness? When and why did they begin to perceive themselves as in part determined by nature, in part directed by society, and in part propelled by their own volition? Can we remain viable as members of a species, as

41. See, for instance, Ernst Robert Curtius, *European Literature and the Latin Middle Ages*, trans. Willard R. Trask (Princeton: Bollingen–Princeton University Press, 1973), pp. 138–44 on the world as a stage and pp. 319–26 on nature as a book. Curtius also mentions (p. 141) that Calderon, who dramatized the concept of the "great theater of the world" in a religious drama by that title, uses the very phrase "gran teatro del mundo" in one of his best-known secular plays whose title in turn invokes the third topos—*Life Is a Dream* (*La vida es sueño*).

participants in a culture, and as responsible selves if we fail to increase our present degrees of existential congruence, cultural consensus, and experiential coherence? Such questions are clearly relevant to the concerns of this book. In chapters 4 and 5, I indeed speculate about both the past and the future of our "self-completing" species.[42] For the moment, let me sketch two alternative or, more likely, complementary genealogies. On the one hand, discourse may well owe its three dimensions as something done, made, and meant to the social, natural, and personal types of worlds that we inhabit as role players, organisms, and selves. On the other hand, we may well be prompted by the second-, third-, and first-personal orientations of verbal practice to experience human existence as social, natural, and personal—a simultaneous being with, of, and toward the world. In either case, as long as our children and their descendants continue to exist as speaking, writing, and thinking organisms, they can hardly leave behind the intersubjective, objective, and subjective dimensions of human existence that verbal doing, making, and meaning at once reflect and help constitute.

Future inquirers into such matters will be well advised to pay increasing attention to postliterate, even postverbal, developments in postmodern communication, representation, and expression. The oral, mental, and written paradigms of modern cultural practice have more than begun to change already: much of our once face-to-face talking is conducted at long distance; a great deal of our once personal thinking can be farmed out to computers, and we aspire to rewrite the very book of nature by inscribing designs of human making into its genetic codes. An-

42. I owe the term to Clifford Geertz, who writes: "The toolmaking, laughing, lying animal, man, is also the incomplete—or, more accurately, self-completing—animal. The agent of his own realization, he creates out of his general capacity for the construction of symbolic models the specific capabilities that define him." See Clifford Geertz, "Ideology as Cultural System," in his *The Interpretation of Cultures: Selected Essays* (New York: Basic Books, 1973), p. 218. The sentences just quoted clearly apply to human individuals of both genders as well as to our species as a whole.

other case in point is the ever greater legal, economic, and psychological impact of television on human action, production, and mentation: the broadcasting of videotaped events tends to provide decisive pretrial publicity; artsy commercials create consumer demand for merchandise yet to be manufactured; and computer-generated music videos make our waking and dreaming minds develop new, largely nonverbal patterns and rhythms of internal perception.

Beyond doubt, the relatively recent explosion of recording technologies will continue to influence the very ways we talk and listen, write and read, imagine and recall. New advances in technology can also be expected to alter the ethics and politics, biology and aesthetics, semiotics and hermeneutics of human doing, making, and meaning. As a result the culture, existence, and experience of future men and women (if we may still call them such) could well prove either more or less than three-dimensional in the sense in which it is helpful to distinguish the intersubjective, objective, and subjective dimensions of being human today.

*Chapter Two*

# The Performance, Recording, and Mental Rehearsal of Cultural Transactions

In this chapter I explore the interplay of communication, expression, and representation in cultural practice, which I define broadly as the engagement of human beings in action, production, and signification. I remain particularly concerned with acts of speech—their face-to-face oral execution, their graphic or electronic storage, and their mental preparation or recapitulation. But I also pay considerable attention to nonverbal channels through which communication, expression, and representation move their cultural cargo between, among, and within human individuals. Artistic endeavors in theater, film, music, and architecture, as well as playing competitive games and following maps and recipes, serve to exemplify the interface of doing, making, and meaning in partly verbal and nonverbal cultural practice.

## Discourse between, among, and within Human Beings

There is much in human action, production, and signification that either remains below the threshold of language or goes beyond its confines. Yet most nonverbal cultural activities (e.g., pottery and dance) could not have been initiated, and none could have developed to its present complexity, without being accompanied by the use of words. Small wonder that even archaeologists studying nonverbal artifacts and musicologists focusing on nonverbal sounds readily acknowledge the great importance of language in all cultural practice.

It is tempting to draw close parallels (as I did in the previous chapter) between the communicative, expressive, and representational functions of culture and the three most familiar media of language use—audible speaking, visible writing, and verbalizable thinking. After all, the predominance of the communicative function goes almost without saying in the intersubjective situations of face-to-face spoken interaction between alternating speakers and listeners. The expressive (not necessarily poetic or otherwise "self-expressive") function in turn prevails when a solitary writer's text—his or her objectified subjectivity—becomes one-directionally effective among distant or, at the time of writing, unborn members of a virtually "universal audience."[1] Finally, the representative function of discourse is most distinctly evinced through the mind's ability to subjectify the objective by turning the outside world into an internal network of categories. In brief, conversations establish links *between*, texts typically circulate *among*, while the mental transactions of perceiving, remembering, and imagining occur *within*, individual human beings.

All the same, the respective cultural functions of face-to-face communication, storable and transportable expression, and men-

1. Cf. Chaïm Perelman and Lucie Obrechts-Tyteca, *The New Rhetoric*, trans. John Wilkinson and Purcell Weaver (Notre Dame, Ind.: University of Notre Dame Press, 1969), pp. 31–35 on "universal audience."

tal representation are not exclusively linked to the oral, written, or mental use of words. For example, while audible speech is the most widespread mode of intersubjective communication, millions of deaf people routinely communicate in one of the world's many gestural sign languages.[2] Likewise, preserving and transporting information does not require its expression in writing: trail markings, fingerprints, photographs, maps, diagrams, audio and video recordings, as well as digitized data in the memory of computers, are familiar instances of knowledge stored by means of nonverbal semiotic systems. Last but not least, some modes of representing the world to ourselves are largely nonverbal (e.g., our musical, chess, pictorial, and mathematical ideas), and the "thinking" farmed out to computers has very little to do with any "natural" language except the computer language teasingly misnamed Natural.

Moreover, speaking, writing, and thinking as we know them are by no means historically constant manifestations of the communicative, expressive, and representational functions of language. In oral cultures, for example, the judge's verdicts and the bard's performances keep reiterating traditions that would have been stored in the texts of former generations, had they produced any. Likewise, the absence of written records like birth and death certificates does not prevent the mental and oral uses of language in unlettered civilizations from expressing each generation's vital connectedness to the worlds of its ancestors and descendants. One could even say that a certain kind of textuality raises its embryonic head in alliteration, rhyme, standard epithets, conventional similes, and other mnemonic devices employed to facilitate the public oral reiteration of community-shaping discourses. The proverbs, divine injunctions, and formulaic ancestral histories preserved in the Hebrew Bible are in fact prototextual instances of nonspontaneous speech characteristic of oral traditions. I also

2. For scholarly treatments of this fascinating subject, consult the extensive bibliography in Oliver Sacks, *Seeing Voices: A Journey into the World of the Deaf* (note 29 to chapter 1).

take it as a sign of the growing but still challengeable authority of written communication that Deut. 5:22 tells of God's giving Moses the Ten Commandments both in speech and in writing. A presumably earlier source followed in Exod. 20:1 had reported oral dispensation only.

Our postliterate age once again blurs the borderlines between speech and writing as respective prime media of instantaneous reciprocal communication and storable one-way expression. Thanks to telephones, radios, and sound recordings, oral utterances—once restricted to face-to-face situations—can depart from the scene of their spatial and temporal origin, while fax machines and electronic mail permit the near-instantaneous exchange of textual messages across long distances. Such technology "freezes" much of the spontaneous flow of formerly spoken discourse into printouts, prerecorded television programs, and other chunks of unidirectional expression; it also "evaporates" a great deal of potential face-to-face communication into a solitary reader's or passive television watcher's unshared mental representation. Invoking the analogy of water, ice, and steam, one could say that speaking, writing, and thinking—the principal liquid, solid, and gaseous states of discourse—permeate our computerized and televising culture in a more or less interchangeable fashion just as the three states of $H_2O$ permeate our physical environment. Consider some recent efforts to enhance the role of dialogue in the very domains of printed and televised discourse. Newspaper and journal editors have been expanding the space devoted to readers' letters and authors' replies, and there is an even greater increase in the airtime devoted to televised phone-in talk shows where government officials and other celebrities orally respond to viewers. Such printed or televised dialogue manages to bottle the intersubjective juices of face-to-face communication and thereby keep conversational exchange from freezing into monological expression. In other words, newspaper columns like "Dear Abby" and television programs like "Larry King Live" share a capacity to maintain at least a semblance of betweenity among us.

*Sound and Image in the Age of Rampant Reproducibility*

Initially, of course, writing and other early methods of cultural recording mainly served to facilitate intersubjective communication between human beings present—or at least personally known—to each other. Even today, the handwritten outline of a speech is often ancillary to oral delivery on a public occasion. By contrast, printed books usually fulfill their cultural function through the mental performances of solitary readers. The printing press has thus increased handwriting's potential for divorcing the product of literate self-expression from the event of a person expressing himself or herself. In the last hundred years or so, photography, phonography, and other forms of mechanical reproduction have joined printing as successful invaders of areas of culture that had formerly been dominated by singular performances or by highly individualized products of self-expression in such arts as painting and sculpture.[3] As a result, today's world is replete with lasting records and manifold replicas of what used to be transitory instances of doing or unique results of making. Indeed, the enhanced importance of typographic, photographic, and electronic recordings often permits culture's representational or expressive function to overshadow its communicative function. Especially in the verbal, acoustic, and gestural realms, much of what used to be intersubjective has thus become either subjectified (as when a silent reader "performs" printed texts or scores for an internal audience of one) or objectified (as when listeners to tapes and movie watchers attend repeatable "playbacks" of prerecorded sounds and sights).[4]

3. Walter Benjamin stresses the political implications of art's modern reproducibility; see the influential essay "The Work of Art in the Age of Mechanical Reproduction," in his *Illuminations,* trans. Harry Zohn (New York: Harcourt, 1968).
4. Graphic notation and electronic recording function quite differently, of course. The following thumbnail characterization of that difference is contextualized in my "Reconceiving Notation and Performance," *Journal of Aesthetic Ed-*

The very possibility of authorial and editorial revision distinguishes texts, musical scores, and other kinds of recordings as instances of solidified expression from the more fluid communication characteristic of a live performance. Even if an author, composer, conductor, or filmmaker should decide to make no revision in the initial draft or initial recording, readers, listeners, or viewers are justified in regarding the final version as deliberately authorized rather than spontaneously improvised.[5] Nonetheless, the absence of the writer's final solidifying review has left some posthumously published works of Marx, Nietzsche, Saussure, and Kafka—to name a few very different authors—intriguingly "fluid."

In most instances, of course, texts, scores, and audio or video recordings do come to us heavily revised either by their initiators or by such "cocreators" as copyeditors, sound technicians, censors, and (more or less error-prone) typesetters. Furthermore, significant parts or even the whole of many electronic recordings are not connected to any live performance at all. This holds not only for music produced on a Moog synthesizer or on equipment of later vintage. The makers of movies and videotapes have also been steadily enlarging their original arsenal of nonperformative techniques like trick photography and cartoon animation. With increasing frequency, motion pictures include computer-generated sounds and images with the result that filmmakers *construct*

---

*ucation* 25 (1991): 53: "While a score or a text is a *semiotic* device for *denoting* a *class* of compliant performances, a phonograph record or videotape is a *technological* device for *storing* a *single* performance, edition, or animation." It should become clear from the ensuing discussion of moviemaking that most products of cinematography store editions rather than actual performances even if the camera captures human performers in its initial recording of sounds and images.

5. An author who revises one part of a text puts a new stamp of approval on the unrevised parts, whose precise function typically changes in their new context. This applies to revisions in a contract or business letter as well as to culturally more prestigious instances of revising (e.g., Wordsworth's alterations of poems he had published earlier).

likeness rather than literally *record* live events by means of a stationary camera and microphone.[6]

Given such advances in technology, it may be useful to map the growing number of major routes currently available for cultural traffic.[7] Some of my "maps" no doubt cover quite familiar ground. Concerning the performance, recording, and mental rehearsal of exclusively verbal transactions, for example, it is well known that our uttered words are typically heard "here and now" even though they can also be heard "there and then"—in principle, anywhere and at any future time—thanks to transmission and recording devices. It is likewise clear that written messages are typically read at a time and place different from the original scene of writing even though they can also be received while being produced (e.g., on a blackboard or on properly interlinked computer monitors). Finally, quasi-verbal thoughts directly occur only to the thinking person even though their occurrence can sometimes be inferred by others (e.g., from symptoms of concealed embarrassment in a liar's speech, writing, or gestural behavior).

Some other aspects of cultural practice have received less frequent systematic attention. For example, one can speak, write, and even think either in one's own name or, as stage performers, speechwriters, and novelists using first-person narrators or free indirect discourse variously do, in invisible quotation marks. To complicate things further, texts may be read by the author, the scribe, or anyone else either silently or aloud, and if they are read

6. See Rick Altman, ed., *Sound Theory Sound Practice* (London: Routledge, 1992), p. 44, on the substitution of "constructed iconicity" for "recorded indexicality." Altman's phrases invoke C. S. Peirce's distinctions between the iconic, indexical, and symbolic modes of signification in *The Philosophy of Peirce: Selected Writings*, ed. Justus Buchler (1944; rpt. New York: Dover, 1955), pp. 98–119.

7. To forestall misunderstandings, I should point out that the ensuing typology aligns nonacoustic face-to-face communication through a gestured sign language with audible speech rather than visible writing and that it refers to "writing" in a broad enough sense to include all production of texts (e.g., court stenography, typing, and typesetting).

aloud, such a "performance" (just like any improvised utterance) may be heard as well as overheard.[8] A text can also be recited from memory or can, if cast in dialogue form, be acted out by several performers who may (just like people "improvising" their conversational roles in everyday life) prove highly inventive in their vocal and gestural behavior. Furthermore, the verbal meanings of a text-based performance, as well as the meanings emerging from ordinary conversations, tend to be supplemented by the nonverbal meanings conveyed through costumes, props, and decor—to use theater terms for the familiar nonverbal accoutrements of virtually all verbal interactions.

To be sure, the sounds and sights of a theatrical performance, just like the sounds and sights of an everyday conversation, can be instantaneously transmitted to another place (e.g., by closed-circuit television). They can also be recorded on film or videotape and then played back any number of times by means of the appropriate equipment. Yet video recordings of a theatrical performance do not give as complete and satisfactory an account of it as audio recordings can give of what really matters in a musical performance. Indeed, most products of "canned" theater make very poor cousins both to printed texts and to live performances, as well as to products of cinematography, about which more anon.

Needless to say, people attending the playback of a recording do not see or hear the same sights or sounds as people attending the visible and audible events that have been recorded. Even spectators at a live performance will perceive quite different sights and sounds depending on where they sit in the auditorium. When it comes to a videotaped version of that perfor-

---

8. It should be noted that I can intend my speech to be heard by persons to whom it is not directly addressed even though those "third parties" indirectly addressed may mistakenly believe that they are merely overhearing it. The same applies to written discourse, where the difference between "hearing" and "overhearing"—between being directly or indirectly addressed and not being addressed by a text or by certain aspects of a text—is further attenuated.

mance, a great deal more depends on camera angles, microphone positions, and a host of variable characteristics of both the recording and the playback equipment and situation. What, then, allows us to regard different playbacks of different recordings as faithful renditions (rather than, say, variations, elaborations, or translations) of a live stage performance or congressional hearing? Our criterion seems to be that an oral or written quotation of what was said in the live event should also count as an oral or written quotation of what is heard in any of the playbacks. In other words, the minimum requirement for talking about different renditions of the *same* event is that a text inscribing the verbal dimension both of the event and of its various recordings should—or might—exist.[9]

The existence of such a text is, however, more frequently potential than actual. As a rule, everyday conversations do not follow preexisting texts and seldom end up being literally transcribed even if they have been electronically recorded. Many stage productions in turn deviate from the published texts of plays, often because no existing text counts as authoritative. Since this is the case with all dramatic works of Shakespeare, even the most bardolatrous director's artistic purposes concerning *Hamlet*, for example, may be best served by minor or not so minor deviations from one of the two early, perhaps "pirated," quarto editions or from one of the many posthumous, "improved" versions beginning with the folio edition of 1623.

Most film adaptations of plays and especially of novels take great liberties with the textual infrastructure of their source. But original movie scripts, too, tend to undergo radical sea change in the process of filming and editing. Indeed, the current technologies employed in the initial recording and subsequent manipulation of images and sounds permit cinemato*graphy* to live up to its

9. I am not concerned here with wordless events and performances (e.g., Marcel Marceau's pantomimes) or with silent movies where the visual medium assimilates to itself whatever verbal material may be present (billboards, subtitles, photographed newspaper headlines, and the like).

name and do its own, special kind of "writing."[10] Outcheating the Greek painter Zeuxis, who reportedly modeled the various parts of his Helen after different maidens, the movies can make us mentally conjoin a filmed face with another person's separately filmed body or an accomplished pianist's hands and performance (prerecorded close-up and sound track) with an unmusical actor shown playing the piano on a distant stage. Dubbing dialogue to procure a more pleasing voice or a more suitable accent is also common. Even documentary films compile their visual and acoustic message from more varied sources than a single unedited shot sequence taken by an immobile camera with a stationary microphone attached to it. What the final product of advanced filmmaking stores for future playbacks is thus not a recorded performance, let alone the recorded performance of a text. Today's typical feature film proffers to the spectators a carefully designed and edited sequence of microevents, each consisting of recorded or computer-generated sounds and sights waiting to be correlated with other sounds and sights by each interpreting member of the audience.

There is a telling difference between theatrical rehearsals and cinematographic takes: rehearsals aim at perfecting a transaction that can henceforth be reenacted; takes aim at producing an object that can henceforth be reproduced. The product orientation of cinematic practice also explains why genuine film scripts yield less "literary" readings than dramatic texts. Apart from the usually sparse stage directions, the playwright's text—like a printed poem or a musical score—can come to life through a series of consecutive moments of a mental performance. By contrast, the entire sequence of instructions given in a film script (just like the whole series of instructions given in a recipe) must be executed before the movie (like a dish) is ready to be served. In other words, film scripts and cookbooks essentially function to guide doing toward making—action toward production. In more than

10. See Altman, *Sound Theory Sound Practice* (note 6 above), p. 44 et passim.

one sense, therefore, film producers make it their business to turn transaction into object, performative process into mass-produced commodity.

Even so, *doing* and *meaning* are by no means eliminated by the filmmakers. To be sure, the products of cinematographic recording largely determine the speed, volume, and most other visual and acoustic features of their proper reception. Yet each attended screening quickly turns footage into brainage—the inert physical "thing made" into a meaningful communicative "act done" to responsive spectators. As moviegoers "concretize" a motion picture's abstract general potential for being experienced, they contribute just as much to the meanings suggested by the final product of filmmaking as theatergoers contribute to the meanings suggested by the transactive doing of a play by live performers.[11]

Close parallels as well as notable contrasts emerge as one compares the verbal and partly verbal practices discussed so far with their nonverbal counterparts. The structural affinity is especially close between discourse and music because text, utterance, and quasi-verbal thought largely correspond to score, performance, and quasi-musical thought. To be sure, musical writing and reading are far less widely practiced in our culture —or in any culture known to me—than the parallel skills of verbal literacy. Yet scores can be performed and performances scored with the same reciprocity we find between the inscribing of verbal utterances and the reading aloud of texts. Also, the electronic recording of discourse and of music will equally preserve the pertinent acoustic features of a particular verbal utterance or musical performance. In a nutshell, musical sounds (just like words) can be acoustically as well as mentally performed and graphically as well as electronically recorded.

Human music does not match the life-sustaining "natural" contribution of nonverbal sounds to the spatial orientation of

11. For Roman Ingarden's view of the reader's role in "concretizing" a literary work, see note 13 to chapter 1.

45

bats, whales, and some other animals.[12] But it has long played important social roles, especially when accompanied by words (as in work songs and war songs) or bodily movements (as in religious rites and communal dancing). Even in the private dimension of being human, the self-addressed speech of children and some adults finds its cognates in such pleasurable habits as humming or whistling in the shower and the corresponding vehicles of private musical self-expression in other cultures.[13] The marked difference between our private and public acts of discourse (and between our private and public acts of music) should encourage exploration of the everyday roots of such macrogenres in sophisticated literary and musical practice as the lyric versus the dramatic, the autobiographical versus the epistolary, the solo versus the ensemble, perhaps even the homophonic versus the polyphonic.

Like the author of words, the composer of music can either perform or inscribe what is in his or her mind. But musical ideas

12. See, however, Doris F. Jonas and A. David Jonas, "Gender Differences in Mental Function: A Clue to the Origin of Language," *Current Anthropology* 16 (December 1975): 626–30, where the authors interestingly speculate about the origin of predominant right-handedness and the corresponding specialization of the left brain hemisphere for intelligent tool and language use. They suggest that the increasingly peltless, itinerant species of early humans needed to carry their offspring rather than trusting them to grab on to the mother's body, and that the soothing effect of the beating heart made it more convenient to carry infants on the left side. If correct, this theory seems to imply that the "natural music" of the heartbeat gave the first impetus to the asymmetrical specialization of our arms and hands as well as to the concomitant and apparently most beneficial separation of crucial functions on different sides of the bicameral human brain.

13. Jean Piaget linked what he called the "egocentric" speech of children to their "original autism" and to Freud's pleasure principle. By contrast, Lev Vygotsky insisted on the ultimately social origin of all speech, including the self-addressed but audible "egocentric" speech of children from which, according to Vygotsky, the "inner speech" of adults—their unuttered but verbalized thinking—evolves. For a concise juxtaposition of the two views, see the editor's introductory essay in Lev Vygotsky, *Thought and Language*, newly revised and edited by Alex Kozulin (Cambridge: MIT Press, 1986), pp. xxxv–xxxvi. I am not aware of a corresponding "debate" concerning the private versus public provenance of music.

more complex than a singable tune or a piece playable on a single instrument cannot be conveyed as easily by the composer's own performance as verbal ideas can be by the author's utterances. For example, the composer's keyboard performance of an opera, even if accompanied by frequent chanting, will hardly approximate in its degree of acoustic equivalence the playwright's solo rendition of dramatic dialogue. Inscribing music, too, is a more laborious process than inscribing verbal discourse: no shorthand musical notation can match the speed, say, of a marching band's live performance.

Acts of collective music making—whether singing around the campfire or playing a Haydn string quartet—may be confined to participants, incidentally overheard by outsiders, or purposely performed for a public. In further likeness to spoken words, musical sounds can be broadcast to distant points in space. By means of either notation or electronic recording, they can also be preserved in time; even the visual aspects of a musical performance can be recorded on videotape. Since no particular record of a musical (or verbal) performance is considered the "real thing," a recording made from another recording is a much more acceptable—and occasionally preferable—substitute for the original recording than painted or photographic reproductions ever can be of an original painting.[14] Tapes, compact discs, and other means of "storing" a performance are thus comparable to photographs, lithographs, prints of engravings, or even printed copies of a text or musical score. They are objects—usually mass-produced from a template, negative matrix, or other nonperformative prototype—that serve as interchangeable "tokens" of the work itself, which in turn counts as their ideal "type."[15]

14. Musical recordings seldom count as genuine substitutes for a live performance, however. This is partly why many people are willing to pay more for concert tickets than for tapes or compact discs containing the entire program in a possibly superior musical interpretation.

15. For an influential technical distinction between token and type, see *Collected Papers of Charles Sanders Peirce* (note 18 to chapter 1), vol. 4, *The Simplest Mathematics* (Cambridge: Harvard University Press, 1933), p. 423. In a more

The playback of a recorded musical performance—just like the playback of a recorded everyday conversation or stage performance—will differ in many ways from the original performance. As with recorded discourse, musical identity across numerous sets of quite different acoustic events thus depends on the approximate compliance of performances and playbacks with an actual or potential "text." And in further likeness to verbal practice, the ideal type of a musical work may be instantiated in no actual score, or else it may be instantiated in a large number of very different scores as long as each score displays properly arranged tokens of a notational system's distinct graphemic types.[16]

Let me sum up what has transpired so far about verbal, theatrical, musical, and cinematographic transactions. In all four do-

general sense, a musical piece is the ideal type of all faithful scores, performances, recordings, and playbacks of the work. Recordings and playbacks, however, not only are tokens of a particular work (e.g., Mozart's *Jupiter* Symphony) but are also tokens of what might be called a subtype, namely, one of the work's interpretations (e.g., in common parlance, "Bruno Walter's *Jupiter* Symphony"). Nelson Goodman's otherwise useful distinctions between allographic and autographic arts and between singular and multiple arts do not explicitly address audio or video recording; cf. *Languages of Art* (Indianapolis: Bobbs-Merrill, 1968), pp. 99–123.

16. In "Reconceiving Notation and Performance" (see note 4 above) I point out that we encounter both texts and scores in diverse manifestations of an ideal set of graphemic types; cf. esp. p. 49: "There are just about as many ways to write or print the grapheme 'p' as there are ways to utter or electronically synthesize the corresponding phoneme." The same holds for the graphemic units of musical scores to which the quasi-phonemic acoustic units of musical performances are judged to have complied according to the conventions of antecedent semiotic and hermeneutic practice. In the same article I advocate the relaxation of Nelson Goodman's strict external criteria of identical spelling and error-free acoustic execution as prerequisites for "work identity" (pp. 51–52): "Some inscriptions of a work contain typographic errors, while others reflect the historical evolution of notational conventions; some performances are mistake-ridden, while others employ verbal dialects or musical instruments unknown to the author or composer. . . . The strenuously maintained textual 'identity' of most classical and many modern works therefore rests at least as much on critical interpretation and historical scholarship as on accurate copying and careful proofing. Likewise, the experienced mind matters more in our search for work-identical musical performance than the untutored, naked ear."

mains, live performance by one or more persons may be attended by nonperformers whose presence is not necessarily known to the performers; the performance can be improvised, read aloud from text or score, or executed from memory; it can be recorded graphically or by various electronic devices, some of which also enable instantaneous transmission from one place to another; it can be rehearsed mentally from text, script, score, or memory; it can also be played back from a film reel or other kind of recording; and finally it can be dispensed with altogether because a particular verbal, theatrical, musical, or filmic event may never leave the page or its initiator's mind and because some modes of recording (e.g., the production of animated cartoons or electronic music) do not involve live performance at all.

## The Multitemporality of Arts, Crafts, and Games

Any inscription (verbal, musical, choreographic, etc.) can either preexist or memorialize performance; some inscriptions will do both. Likewise, we can mentally anticipate as well as recollect performances of various kinds. It is no doubt hard to have a complete mental experience of an entire play or symphony without recourse to text or score. But shorter verbal or musical sequences often occur to a person or are recalled in the absence of concurrent perceptual prompting. Thus the three verbal media considered in chapter 1—spoken, written, and mental discourse—find their full set of analogues in music and some other arts (e.g., performed, choreographed, and mentally envisioned dance) as well. Indeed, performance (including live enactment, attended playback, and silent reading), recording (including graphic notation and electronic reproduction), and mentation (including both recollection and invention) can be considered the three principal guises that works of the so-called temporal arts may don.

To be sure, remembered and imagined instances of cultural practice take place *within* individuals, whereas graphically or electronically recorded cultural transactions tend to circulate *among* them. Yet both the subjective *meaning*, by a mind, of remembered or imagined words, sounds, and images and the objective *making*, by one or more producers, of texts, scores, films, and other recordings presuppose some of the intersubjective *doings* (e.g., conversations, staged performances, orchestra rehearsals, public screenings, etc.) associated with verbal, musical, and cinematographic practice. Furthermore, subjectified representations in memory or the imagination, as well as objectified expressions like texts, scores, and videotapes, can always turn through public performance into intersubjective communication *between* "senders" and "receivers" of culture.[17]

The interchange between making and doing (product and process, or object and transaction) is less frequently noted in painting, sculpture, and architecture than in verbal or musical practice. But action and signification are by no means completely eclipsed by production and reproduction in the so-called atemporal visual arts either. The massive things made in architectural practice, for example, owe their objective existence to the intersubjective doing involved with their original construction and subsequent preservation. Furthermore, they owe their particular place in intersubjective culture to the subjective experiences of many individual indwellers and onlookers. Even the initial temporal "execution" of a spatial plan through construction deserves more theoretical attention than it usually receives. But the most unduly neglected kind of architectural transaction is the "imple-

---

17. The communicative relationship *between* live performers and audience can remain predominant even if an essential part of what the audience hears has been prerecorded. Such is the case when well-timed playbacks of electronic music supplement the live sounds of a symphony orchestra or when a lip-synching singer's earlier recording becomes audible at the time of his or her "live" performance. Whitney Houston's rendition of "The Star Spangled Banner" at the 1991 Super Bowl is an example of such lip-synching; for details and analysis see Steve Wurtzler, " 'She Sang Live, but the Microphone Was Turned Off': The Live, the Recorded, and the *Subject* of Representation," in *Sound Theory Sound Practice*, ed. Rick Altman (note 6 above), esp. pp. 87–88.

menting" of buildings—the performative process of "making them work" as inhabited human dwellings.[18] We constantly interact with the structured spaces in which we live, work, play, worship, or otherwise abide. By thus realizing the transactive potential of a building, we perform it, so to speak, just as musicians perform a score or reciters of a verbal inscription perform a text. The long stretches of unobserved "solo performance" of a room or building by a lone occupant are in fact comparable to silent readings of a text or score by a solitary person. Visiting a pyramid or cathedral is a much more public and rather complex affair. After all, a pyramid or cathedral does not simply express the architectural ideas of its (typically multiple and anonymous) "author." Along with that objectifying expression, the intersubjective efforts of the monument's actual "producers" and the subjectifying sentiments of its previous "consumers" also invite empathic or ironic mental reenactment by any person entering or circumambulating the building. By spending time inside structures we thus have the capacity to perform both their material space and their cultural history. But even viewing works of architecture from the outside—just like the visual crisscrossing of a work of sculpture, painting, or interior decorating—transfuses subjective time into physical objects.

18. I borrow Nelson Goodman's helpful distinction between the execution and implementation of artworks from his *Of Mind and Other Matters* (Cambridge: Harvard University Press, 1984), p. 143: "Execution consists of making a work, implementation of making it work." Goodman illustrates the difference between execution and implementation as follows: "The novel is completed when written, the painting when painted, the play when performed. But the novel left in the drawer, the painting stacked in a storeroom, the play performed in an empty theater does not fulfill its function. In order to work, the novel must be published in one way or another, the painting shown publicly or privately, the play presented to an audience" (p. 142). Goodman might agree with me that a building seen but not entered "works," at best, as an oversize sculpture. But my general view of what it takes to "implement" buildings and other artworks is likely to strike his stricter followers as too mentalistic. Cf. my "Reconceiving Notation and Performance" (note 4 above), esp. pp. 48–52, and Catherine Z. Elgin, "What Goodman Leaves Out," *Journal of Aesthetic Education* 25 (1991): 93–94 esp.

A transfusion of subjective time is also required by literary texts because they are sequential rather than genuinely temporal: a text may guide but cannot determine the tempo of its voiced or silent reading. Texts are comparable to maps in leaving speed an undetermined variable while indicating the sequence in which the points between departure and destination should be covered. To be sure, the adjacent segments of a text are typically designed to be read from beginning to end—in their entirety and in a specified direction. By contrast, a map (like a painting) can be visually crisscrossed in an idiosyncratic fashion, and the territory charted on it can be "performed" by a traveler both partially and in more than one direction. To continue with the same analogy, many readers employ the psychological equivalent of a car's cruise control during their encounter with almost any type of written discourse. Our failure to read different texts (and different parts of the same text) at different speeds often leads to hermeneutic accidents on the busy highways of textual traffic. Indeed, many disagreements about the meaning of a text result from the different speeds at which the disagreeing readers perused the text in question. As I put it elsewhere, we should not assume that an account of the erudite professor's painstakingly thorough reading experience is necessarily relevant to the "story" that a faster, nonprofessional reading might elicit from the same "discourse."[19]

In contrast to the largely optional tempo of the individual mental performance of poems and novels, a certain speed of delivery must be intersubjectively agreed upon if several people participate in a dramatic or musical performance. Small wonder that musical scores often include precise metronomic instructions (or at least approximations like "andante" or "presto") even for their silent, "subjective" performance. As a final step in the same direc-

19. See Paul Hernadi, "On the How, What, and Why of Narrative," *Critical Inquiry* 7 (1980): 202; reprinted in W. J. T. Mitchell, *On Narrative* (Chicago: University of Chicago Press, 1981), p. 198, and Seymour Chatman, *Story and Discourse: Narrative Structure in Fiction and Film* (Ithaca: Cornell University Press, 1978).

tion, motion pictures and other kinds of video and audio recordings unequivocally prescribe the speed at which the playback
equipment should run. All the same, a great deal of postproduc-
tion interference tends to occur with the objective temporality of
recordings, for both subjective and intersubjective reasons. Just
like teachers of film studies courses, many people renting videotapes often stop and restart, repeat, skip, speed up, slow down, or
otherwise manipulate the sounds and sights of a particular playback. Even recordings fail thus to reduce the multitemporality of
cultural practice to anything like the irreversible and even flow of
time presupposed in Newtonian physics.[20] But no actual manipulation of the equipment is needed for each attended playback to
occur at the human junction of subjective, intersubjective, and objective times.

Time is always perceived and conceived by individual persons
within their social and natural settings. Hence caution is advised
whenever one thinks, talks, or writes about any aspect or variety of
time as fundamentally individual, social, or natural. Nonetheless,
some phenomena much more than others do involve time as
chiefly subjective, intersubjective, or objective: the succession of
images in a dream, the succession of differently structured and

20. We do well to remember that Newton had to defend his innovative concept of "absolute, true, mathematical time," now also challenged by relativity
theory and quantum physics, against "relative, apparent, and common" times
(cf. Donald J. Wilcox, *The Measure of Times Past: Pre-Newtonian Chronologies and
the Rhetoric of Relative Time* (Chicago: University of Chicago Press, 1987). Seven
decades after Newton's death, Johann Gottfried Herder's *Metakritik* (1799) of
Kant's *Critique of Pure Reason* (1781) pitted a radically plural view of times
against the attempt to homogenize multiple temporalities into an a priori intuition of absolute time: "Strictly speaking, everything transient has the measure
of *its* time within itself; that measure would endure even if nothing else existed.
. . . There are in the universe countless times at any one time. . . . The measure
and scope of *all* times is a figment of the imagination [*Wahnbild*]." My translation from Herder's *Metakritik zur Kritik der reinen Vernunft* (Berlin: Aufbau,
1955), pp. 68–69. For fuller citation and commentary see my "Objective, Subjective, Intersubjective Times: Guest Editor's Introduction," *Time and Society* 1
(May 1992): 147–58, from which the first three sentences of the next paragraph
have been adopted.

valued days in a week, and the succession of darkness and light in a day may serve as relatively noncontroversial examples of predominantly personal, social, and natural temporalities. In a similar fashion, our respective practices of mental representation, face-to-face communication, and durable expression are predominantly linked to the personal time of subjective experience (Bergson's *durée*), to the social time of intersubjective culture, and to the natural time of objective existence (Bergson's *temps*, whose steady progress is frozen into detemporalized sequence in physical objects like books and tapes).[21] Yet no cultural practice reduces one kind of time to another. For example, the oral use of language does not eliminate our subjective flux of mental time but coordinates different private temporalities within the intersubjective temporal horizon of a face-to-face verbal encounter. Likewise, the objective linear sequence of written language detaches itself from its writer's subjective time and from the intersubjective time of the writer's lifeworld, but it remains insertable into its reader's subjective time and into the intersubjective time of the reader's lifeworld.

The proliferation of recordings and playbacks in our postliterate culture has led to an unprecedented confluence of multiple spaces and times in many moments of ordinary experience. We listen to music, prerecorded in a studio or concert hall, while driving on a freeway or reading in a living room. Or we attend to the evening news, full of live or prerecorded reports from halfway across the globe, while fixing dinner. Speaking of dinner, our very meals tend to be prepared at the temporal crossroads of a radically "heterochronous" world.[22] Cooking a dish according

21. For Bergson's first statement, in 1889, of the difference between the *temps* of Newtonian physics and experienced *durée*, see Henri Bergson, *Time and Free Will: An Essay on the Immediate Data of Consciousness*, trans. F. L. Pogson (London: Allen and Unwin, 1910). On "social time" and on "time as a social fact," see Barbara Adam, *Time and Social Theory* (Philadelphia: Temple University Press, 1990), esp. pp. 42–45.

22. The term "heterochronous" has been suggested by one of Mikhail Bakhtin's recent interpreters, see Gary Saul Morson, "Bakhtin, Genres, and Temporality," *New Literary History* 22 (1991): 1085.

to a printed recipe amounts to something like a culinary performance comparable to a pianist's (present) sight-reading of a
(past) musical composition. More pertinent still, the use of frozen
or canned food (especially when a multidish TV dinner gets
heated up in a computerized microwave oven) is a rough gastro-
nomic equivalent of the playback from a compact disc of the
"canned" performance of musical pieces composed by different
people at different times. There are still occasions for convivial
doing rather than more or less depersonalized making in the
realm of nutrition. For example, some Japanese restaurants the-
atricalize cooking, to the visual, acoustic, and olfactory delight of
the feasting "audience." Likewise, grilling hot dogs and ham-
burgers at a picnic while the first round of sandwiches is being
eaten brings the space and time of cooking and of feasting into
transactive proximity. By sharp contrast, the mass production of
powdered milk and other kinds of baby food objectifies much of
the transactive process of cross-generational nurturing.

Such fanciful analogies aside, the widespread use of computerized cooking appliances exemplifies a general trend in the (so far
three-phased) evolution of nutritional practices. A clear-sighted
history of human alimentation would need to note that the *actions*
of our hunting and gathering forebears were largely superseded
by the *production* of crops and livestock in agricultural communities whose indispensable tools (from plows and lassos to tractors
and electric cattle prods) must be manufactured according to the
*signification* of increasingly complex spoken, written, or printed
instructions. In today's postindustrial West, a great deal of food is
prepared and almost all food is distributed by the so-called ser-
vice industries. These indispensable but, strictly speaking, non-
productive processors and dispatchers of nourishment rely on
computerized inventories to meet consumer demands generated
in part by staged, pseudodocumentary television commercials.
We can thus discern the preponderance first of doing, then of
making, and finally of meaning with current emphasis, in the
last-named domain, on artificial intelligence and simulated rep-

resentation. An analogous sequence in the respective ascendancy of doing, making, and meaning—from speech through writing to ever more mentalized signification—can be observed in the history of trade. The largely oral communication involved in bartering with actual goods first gave way to exchanges involving coins, banknotes, personal checks, and similar instruments whose abstract monetary value is expressed by what is stamped, printed, or written on them. By now, of course, we typically buy and sell through computerized credit-card accounts and other ghostly agencies of postliterate representation.

The first large "cultural revolution" leading from the preponderance of speech and action to that of writing and production proved progressive on most counts. As Jack Goody has noted, writing makes "skepticism and disagreement articulate and therefore cumulative," thereby increasing "the likelihood of change" because "literate traditions of dissent open up vistas of alternative forms of human organization."[23] I am far less sanguine about the socially activating potential of today's general shift from writing and production to those modes of mentation and signification that are favored by the postliterate media. In particular, the current flood of televised information seems to work toward dissipating both reformist and conservative social agendas of intersubjective doing. To be sure, the television

23. See Goody's entry "Time: Social Organization," in *International Encyclopedia of the Social Sciences* (New York: Macmillan, 1968), 16:40. It should be noted that Goody's later comparisons between orality and literacy became critical of "ethnocentric dichotomies that have characterized social thought in the period of European expansion." Jack Goody, *The Domestication of the Savage Mind* (Cambridge: Cambridge University Press, 1977), p. 9. Many subsequent authors discussing such matters are even more eager than Goody to avoid broadly based generalizations about cultures as supposedly either literate/rational/advanced/abstract or oral/mythic/primitive/concrete. See, for instance, Brian Street, *Literacy in Theory and Practice* (Cambridge: Cambridge University Press, 1984); Ruth Finnegan, *Literacy and Orality: Studies in the Technology of Communication* (Oxford: Blackwell, 1988); and the chapter "Literacy and Orality" in Rosalind Thomas, *Literacy and Orality in Ancient Greece* (Cambridge: Cambridge University Press, 1992). My own concern here is with what writing *can* do rather than what, supposedly always, it *will* or *must* do.

viewer's eyes and ears are afforded a degree of spatial and temporal diversity that used to be available only through memory and the imagination. Yet our increasing sensory preoccupation with a semiotically saturated present tends to narrow the span of our spatial and temporal attention. Bombarded by the visual and acoustic signs of the postliterate media, we are often riveted to present semiotic "meaning" in lieu of significant engagement with products of past material "making" and future-oriented acts of social "doing."[24] With enormous amounts of material production and ideological signification going on around us, the most typical world-altering action routinely performed in the remote-controlled pluriverse of cable television may well be changing channels.

A great deal of passive television viewing is "done," so to speak, by couch potatoes who vicariously identify with athletes engaged in fiercely competitive but, from society's vantage point, rather inconsequential actions. Barring serious injuries, ball games clearly sublimate the brute facts of intersubjective struggle into rule-governed play. Yet in the spirit of radical contestation, no one person or team can determine the entire course of a sporting event. Even the most lopsided basketball game, for example, emerges from the confluence of two sets of collective projects locked in battle. The attempted execution of every game plan proceeds against at least one opposing plan as if two or more different musical scores were trying to drown each other out during a single performance.

The basic situation is quite similar in chess—a game of individual rather than communal, mental rather than physical, contest.

24. Sometimes it takes great effort to discover how today's general super-abundance of mental signification (Baudrillard speaks of a make-believe hyper-reality of simulacra and simulations) is intertwined with specific circumstances of material production and social action. See Jean Baudrillard, "Simulacra and Simulations" (1981) in *Selected Writings*, ed. Mark Poster (Cambridge: Polity, 1988), pp. 166–84, and (for a critical view of Baudrillard) Christopher Norris, *What's Wrong with Postmodernism* (Baltimore: Johns Hopkins University Press, 1990), esp. pp. 164–93.

To be sure, after a succession of moves has been "performed" by two players or two computers, chess fans can *make* copies of the score sheet, *do* the moves on their own boards, and *mean*—mentally reenact—the strategies and tactics of the game just as one can copy, play, or recall a piece of music. Yet only in retrospect does a chess game emerge as a single, unified performance. While the game is in progress, it is always antagonistically improvised, as it were, by two disparate sets of intentions.

Chess is sometimes called an art, but its basically combative character is revealed through a significant difference between musical and chess notation, namely, how each deals with the temporal aspect of the action it records. A musical score specifies the relative time allotted to each recorded unit even in the absence of any numerical or verbal indication of the speed with which the piece in question should be performed. For example, a quarter note is expected to take about half as long to perform as an adjacent half note. By contrast, the individual chess moves inscribed on a scoring sheet do not specify the time it originally took to plan and execute them; nor does the scoring sheet specify the time it should take chess fans studying the game to reenact particular moves. The emphasis is clearly on how the two sides manage to counter each other's objectives irrespective of the time that elapses while they do so. At further distance from musical notation, the final "score" of a basketball game is completely oriented toward result rather than progress. It fails to indicate the sequence (let alone the temporal duration) of the individual scoring events or to reflect the strategically crucial "time out" periods.

Both in basketball and in chess, the entire visible action might be continuously recorded by a stationary camera, but the resulting record would not do justice to what makes basketball basketball and chess chess. The effective broadcasting of a basketball game highlights whatever is essential to the ongoing struggle through frequent use of close-ups, changing camera angles, slow-motion playbacks, and a great deal of verbal commentary. The most appropriate way of televising chess games in turn involves several demonstration boards on which expert commentators, at a considerable distance from the competing players, offer instant analyses of the moves that have been made, may soon be made, or could have been made. The actual moves are usually received in the studio by phone or teletype without any pictures being transmitted of the physical actions performed by the grand masters.

References to previous games in the respective sports constitute a necessary part of properly "covering" a particular basketball or chess event. After all, the lore of past games—a manifold of stories about the ongoing history of a given type of cultural practice—helps to determine the meaning and significance of current transactions. Indeed, the intersubjective dimension of agreed-upon conventions—comparable to the role of certain overarching traditions of representation, expression, and communication in the arts—is the defining one in most games. For example, you can play chess with vastly different (objective) pieces and according to vastly different (subjective) strategies. But if you bent or broke the (intersubjective) rules of chess without securing the consent of at least some players, you would find yourself in an altogether different game or, more likely, in no game at all. Which brings us back to verbal communication—the practice of serious "language games" in which most social competition and cooperation is transacted according to grammatical, rhetorical, and logical rules reflecting shared "forms of life."[25] We now turn to a particularly significant set of such games—the language games being played when we say "we" and thereby draft ourselves and other individuals into communities looking to compete or cooperate with other teams of players.

25. Cf. section 23 of Ludwig Wittgenstein, *Philosophical Investigations* (note 28 to chapter 1), p. 11: "the term 'language-*game*' is meant to bring into prominence the fact that the *speaking* of language is part of an activity, or of a form of life."

# Chapter Three

# Who We Are: The Rhetoric, Grammar, and Logic of Communal Identities

Vice President Dan Quayle's difficulty with the word "potato" introduced spelling as an issue in the 1992 United States presidential campaign. But the political year's hottest potato may well have been the rhetorically correct use of pronouns. Recall that Ross Perot decided to quit the race for several months just after he had drawn fire for addressing his predominantly black audience at the NAACP convention with phrases like "you people" and "your people." By contrast, Bill Clinton's popularity rating soared after he had declared in his acceptance of the Democratic Party's nomination: "This is America. There is no 'them' here. There is only us." Small wonder if, by the time of the first televised debate of the three major presidential candidates, Perot joined the other two in stressing that "we're all stuck here together" and that "our differences are our strength."

The proper use of "we" and related words like "us," and "ourselves" has recently become the focus of academic discussion well beyond the sphere of professional linguists. The philosopher Richard Rorty, for example, defines moral progress as the ability to see "more and more traditional differences (of tribe, religion, race, customs, and the like)" as relatively unimportant and to "think of people wildly different from ourselves as included in the range of 'us.'"[1] Radical critics of Rorty's self-declared "bourgeois liberal" stance in turn object to the rhetoric of expressions like "we Americans" or "human beings like us." In her plea for a "democratic-socialist-feminist pragmatism," the philosopher Nancy Fraser charges that "Rorty homogenizes social space, assuming, tendentiously, that there are no deep social cleavages capable of generating conflicting solidarities and opposing 'we's.'"[2] In a comparable spirit, the literary critic Marianna Torgovnick faults some proponents of the Western cultural tradition for their habitual use of "we" as a "covert, and sometimes coercive, universal."[3] Even the anthropologist Clifford Geertz, who does not accuse overeager "we"-sayers of coercive homogenizing, challenges the notion of a universal human community when he praises ethnography's bent to place "particular

1. Richard Rorty, *Contingency, Irony, and Solidarity* (Cambridge: Cambridge University Press, 1989), p. 192.

2. Nancy Fraser, "Solidarity or Singularity? Richard Rorty between Romanticism and Technocracy," in *Reading Rorty*, ed. Alan R. Malachowski (Oxford: Blackwell, 1990), pp. 314–16. A similar critique of a British conservative speaker's casual use of "we" can be found in Michael Billig, "Very Ordinary Life and the Young Conservatives," in *Getting into Life*, ed. Halla Beloff (London: Methuen, 1986), pp. 86–90. It is interesting, however, that a rhetorical analysis of some French political tracts of May 1968 draws the following conclusion: "The left show a predilection for 'nous,' and the right for 'vous,'" even though, in addressing a public that could not be assumed to be uniformly sympathetic to either side, "it is the left who emphasize struggle, while the right will stress consensus, universality, and themes of national and public interest." See Gill Seidel, "Ambiguity in Political Discourse," in *Political Language and Oratory in Traditional Society*, ed. Maurice Bloch (London: Academic Press, 1975), p. 223.

3. Marianna Torgovnick, "The Politics of the 'We,'" *South Atlantic Quarterly* 91 (1992): 49. I regret that this insightful discussion takes as its point of departure a textual example where, as Torgovnick knows, the translator has substituted "we" for the generic pronoun *man* ("one") occurring in the German original.

we-s among particular they-s, and they-s among we-s, where all
... already are, however uneasily."[4]

Now, Perot's consequential choice of the pronoun "you"
merely signaled in grammatical terms that he was talking *to* the
members of his audience (rather than *for* or *about* them). All the
same, the rhetoric of his "you people" struck many listeners and
commentators as revealing a distanced or even condescending attitude. The disparate political reactions to Perot's "you" and Clinton's "we," along with the widespread anxiety as to the proper
use of "we" in current academic discourse,[5] highlight the need
for examining the grammar, rhetoric, and logic of the pronominal
shaping of communal identities. In the three parts of this chapter—a mere sketch of the complex issues involved—I proceed as
follows. First I consider the use of "we" and kindred pronouns
from the grammatical vantage point of the relevant options available in particular languages. Next I address the same topic from
the rhetorical vantage point of the intended or actual effects of ex-
ercising those options in particular situations. Finally, I explore
the logic of the pronominal shaping of communal identities independent of the particular languages and situations in and
through which particular instances of such shaping occur. My
own concepts of grammar, rhetoric, and logic have, of course,
evolved in the specific context of the languages that I know or
know of and with respect to such situations as I have been socialized to inhabit. But the general definitions of grammar, rhetoric,
and logic implied here reflect the respective focus of most grammarians, rhetoricians, and logicians on well-formed verbal ex-

4. Clifford Geertz, "The Uses of Diversity," *Michigan Quarterly Review* 25
(1986): 119, 112.
5. The perceived need to be defensive about one's "we"-saying is expressed by a literary critic whose recent disclaimer I wish to echo on my own
behalf: "The reader ought not to be alarmed, or nasty, about my repeated use
of the first-person plural to discuss the other pronoun positions. . . . I use the
'we' and 'us' proleptically—that is, to refer to whomever [*sic*] manages provi-
sionally to identify with them." See Charles Altieri, "Life after Difference: The
Positions of the Interpreter and the Positionings of the Interpreted," *Monist* 73
(1990): 292 n. 1.

pression, effective interpersonal communication, and coherent conceptual representation.[6]

## The Grammar of Saying "We"

Language as such does not make it easy to tell who we are. The singular pronouns of the first, second, and third persons establish in principle that *I* am speaking or writing to *you* about *him*, *her*, or *it*. Yet the referents of "I" and "you" vary according to just who addresses whom on a particular occasion, while the identity of the referents of "he," "she," and "it" can depend on either linguistic or extralinguistic context. Even less clear is the pronominal indication of the number of persons cast in the respective roles of sender(s), intended receiver(s), and other mentioned constituent(s) of a message. Modern English, for example, appears to care so little about just how many people hear or read a message that it provides "you" as the only second-person form of pronominal address regardless of the number of intended receivers. *Vous* and *Sie*, the French and German equivalents of "you" in formal second-person address, are also used for both singular and plural referents, while Korean and a few other languages lack distinct plural pronouns in both the second and the third person.

By contrast, every known language seems to have developed grammatical or even lexical means for distinguishing the single

6. In two recent papers I have interrelated grammar, rhetoric, and logic in a more explicitly contemporary fashion; see "Coverage and Discovery: The Case for Detrivializing the Trivium," *ADE Bulletin* 89 (spring 1988): 38–40, and *"Ratio* Contained by *Oratio*: Northrop Frye on the Rhetoric of Nonliterary Prose," in *Visionary Poetics: Essays on Northrop Frye's Criticism*, ed. Robert D. Denham and Thomas Willard (New York: Lang, 1991). Needless to say, many card-carrying logicians exclude most issues raised in the third section of this chapter from the purview of their discipline, which they want to limit to the impersonal (in fact, third-personal) dimension of thought. By contrast, I see "grammar" (the systematized habits of verbal expression) and "logic" (the conceptual ordering of representable experience) interlinked in the multiperson domain of rhetorical situations.

sender of a message (in English, "I") from a group of people that typically includes the sender and to which group the message refers by some equivalent of "we."[7] Yet the conventional assumption that "we" is the plural of "I" remains unsupported by a careful look at grammatical form. Even languages whose plural pronouns in the second or third person are conspicuously related to the corresponding singulars (French *il/ils*, for example) tend to have an etymologically distinct pronoun for what often is—but should not be—called "first-person plural" (e.g., *nous*—unrelated to *je*).[8] Likewise, the disparate referential functioning of "I" and "we" and of their equivalents in other languages makes it plain

7. The distinction need not be expressed through pronouns (e.g., the difference in Latin between *amo* and *amamus* suffices to differentiate between "I love" and "we love"), but it may also require double expression (e.g., through pronouns and verb endings as in German *ich liebe* and *wir lieben*). My sweeping generalization concerning "every known language" is based on Paul Forchheimer, *The Category of Person in Language* (Berlin: Walter de Gruyter, 1953), and David Ingram, "Typology of Personal Pronouns," in *Universals of Human Language*, ed. Joseph H. Greenberg, vol. 3, *Word Structure* (Stanford: Stanford University Press, 1978). I am not aware of any challenge to their pertinent findings, even though Forchheimer's book was criticized on other grounds in reviews by Fred W. Householder Jr. (*Language* 31 [January–March 1955], 93–100) and Dell Hymes (*International Journal of American Linguistics* 21 [July 1955]: 294–300). See also the more recent general statement in Stephen R. Anderson and Edward L. Keenan's chapter "Deixis," in *Language Typology and Syntactic Description*, vol. 3, *Grammatical Categories and the Lexicon*, ed. Timothy Shopen (Cambridge: Cambridge University Press, 1985), p. 263: "Apparently, all languages make a morphemic distinction between a first person singular pronoun ('I') and at least one first person plural form ('we')."

8. The contrasting French first-person forms *je/nous* (as opposed to the identical *vous/vous* in the formal version of second-person address and to the "pluralized" masculine and feminine third-person forms *il/ils, elle/elles*) may serve as Indo-European examples; the Hungarian pair *én/mi* (first person) as opposed to *te/ti* (second person) and *ő/ők* (third person) is a Finno-Ugrian illustration I can attest to as a native speaker. Also in Hopi, representing a completely different language family, *nu'* ("I") and *itam* ("we") are very distinct whereas the second-person singular and plural forms (*um* and *uma*) appear to be related; see Eckehart Malotki, "Hopi Person Deixis," in *Here and There: Cross-linguistic Studies in Deixis and Demonstration*, ed. Jürgen Weissenborn and Wolfgang Klein (Amsterdam: Benjamins, 1982), p. 224. All but a handful of the seventy-one languages examined by Forchheimer (see note 7 above) have an equivalent of "we" that is lexically independent from their equivalent of "I."

that "we" is not simply the plural form of "I." For example, the referent of "I" in "I have been working very hard" is clearly the sender of the verbal message, but the range of reference for "we" in "We have been working very hard" can be quite vague, since the latter sentence is seldom uttered or inscribed by several speakers or writers at the same time.[9] And "we" tends to give us further referential trouble as to just who "we" are. European languages, as well as many others, do not employ different pronouns to indicate whether the receiver(s) of a message are included among or excluded from the referents of the "we" in question.[10] Thus the English sentence, "We'll have dinner in a few minutes," some-

9. Communal chanting is one of the rare modes of verbal expression in which the same words are uttered simultaneously by several people. Interestingly enough, the ancient Greek literary employment of such chanting makes the chorus alternate in its use of "I" and "we" as pronouns of self-reference. Maarit Kaimio, *The Chorus of Greek Drama within the Light of the Person and Number Used* (Helsinki: Societas Scientiarum Fennica, 1970), explores the often unclear rationale for the grammatical shifts in specific plays.

10. The encounter with Native American languages expressing different meanings of "we" through different grammatical elements has obviously stimulated Western interest in this subject. The pertinent terms "exclusive" and "inclusive," distinguishing the respective equivalents of English "we" according to whether they exclude or include the person(s) addressed in their range of reference, first appear in Spanish print in 1603; see M. J. Hardman-de-Bautista, "Early Use of Inclusive/Exclusive," *International Journal of American Linguistics* 38 (1972): 145–46. Among students of non-European languages the very notion that there are only three grammatical persons has not gone unchallenged. For example, A. Akmajian and S. R. Anderson, "On the Use of the Fourth Person in Navajo, or Navajo Made Harder," *International Journal of American Linguistics* 36 (1970): 1–8, C. F. Hockett, "What Algonquian Is Really Like," *International Journal of American Linguistics* 32 (1966): 59–73, and Anderson and Keenan (see note 7 above), pp. 262–63, discuss the occurrence in some languages of what may be considered a fourth or even fifth category of person. As far as I can determine, the categories in question merely subdivide in various ways the realm of things and persons spoken about. By contrast, when the so-called limited inclusive "we" refers to only one sender and one receiver of a verbal message it has a fairly good claim to being the fourth distinct member of the singular pronoun system of a language. Such a pronoun, whose distinct grammatical existence is documented in some languages, completes the fourfold logical system of pronominal possibilities since it conjoins *one sender and one receiver*, while the first person singular refers to *one sender*, the second person singular to *one receiver*, and the third person singular to *one person or object* that is neither sender

65

times invites those to whom it is addressed to get ready for the meal; at other times the same sentence is addressed to one or more persons who need to leave the house or get off the phone at the other end of the line so that *we* may proceed with *our* meal. Indeed, it is possible for someone to hear the words "We'll have dinner in a few minutes" without knowing whether his or her grammatical position with respect to the speaker's "we" is that of a spoken-to second person, a spoken-about third person, or both.

It is hardly surprising that the familiar textbook definition of "we" as "first-person plural" does not carry favor with most serious linguists. In his synoptic *Introduction to Theoretical Linguistics*, John Lyons expresses their more sophisticated view in the following fashion: "The pronoun *we* is to be interpreted as 'I, in addition to one or more other persons'; and the other persons may or may not include the hearer. In other words, *we* is not 'the plural of *I*': rather, it includes a reference to '*I*' and is plural."[11] I am not happy with Lyons's use of "hearer" rather than "addressee" or "intended receiver" because unaddressed third persons (people spoken about by the "we"-sayer) frequently hear what is spoken to someone else about them and because the addressee of a written message is not a hearer at all.[12] More troublesome, however, are some shortcomings of the proposed definition of "we" as "I, in addition to one or more other persons."

On the one hand, "one or more other persons" are not always added to the speaker or writer as referents of "we." The king's

---

nor receiver. See Dell Hymes, *Foundations in Sociolinguistics* (Philadelphia: University of Pennsylvania Press, 1974), p. 165, who notes that, in the Aymara language of Bolivia, this kind of fourth person "is explicitly treated the same" as the familiar first, second, and third singular persons; it is even "taking a plural in exactly the same way."

11. John Lyons, *Introduction to Theoretical Linguistics* (Cambridge: Cambridge University Press, 1969), p. 277.

12. In "Footing," *Semiotica* 25 (1979): 1–29, reprinted in *Forms of Talk* (Philadelphia: University of Pennsylvania Press, 1983), pp. 124–59, Erving Goffman proposed interesting additional refinements of the traditional understanding of the communicative roles played by senders and (addressed or unaddressed) recipients of verbal messages.

"We grieve the death of your brave son" and the author's "We will demonstrate the truth of three propositions" are instances of two kinds of specious plural sometimes called royal (or imperial) and authorial (or editorial).[13] On the other hand, the "I" itself may remain excluded from the range of "we"-reference. The following instances of what I propose to call corporate "we" refer to unaddressed third persons without including any first or second persons—the senders or intended receivers of a verbal message—among their referents: "We are missing too many free throws today" (when spoken by a fan to another fan rather than by a player to another player); "We signed the peace treaty under duress" (when not spoken or written by an actual signatory); "We should have a reliable cancer cure in a hundred years" (when said by an ordinary mortal). In instances of what might be termed custodial "we," the referents are in turn restricted to addressed second persons, as in "How are we feeling today?" (doctor or nurse to patient); "We'll learn the passive voice next week" (German teacher to class); "Let's hurry up with those vegetables" (parent to child); or "Are we dining out tonight?" (butler to employer). In rare instances, a question like "Aren't we cute?" or "Aren't we magnificent?" can refer to an unaddressed third person whose separate pronominal standing as "he" or "she" is temporarily canceled by the speaker. Such use of the pronoun "we"—let's call it adoptive—can occur whether the spoken-about "cute" child or "magnificent" lion, for example, is present at the scene of the utterance or only appears, say, on the television screen.[14]

More will be said in the next section about the rhetorical implications of the royal, authorial, corporate, custodial, and adoptive

13. See, e.g., Otto Jespersen, *A Modern English Grammar on Historical Principles*, part 7, *Syntax*, completed and published by Niels Haislund (Copenhagen: Munksgaard, 1949), p. 269.

14. The existence of the adoptive "we" seems to be ignored by grammarians, perhaps because it tends to occur in what some of them might consider "contracted" rhetorical questions. But "Aren't *we* cute?" hardly derives from "Don't *you* agree with *me* that *she* is cute?" as smoothly as "He *can't seem* to make a living" derives from "He *doesn't seem* to be *able* to make a living" (italics added).

uses of "we." But I wish to stress now that the eleven examples provided in the foregoing paragraph would have to count as grammatically incorrect sentences if the meaning of "we" were defined as "first-person plural" or as Lyons's "I, in addition to one or more other persons." Fortunately, there is no need to subscribe to such a narrow definition. After all, "we" belongs to the extended family of protean words like "here" and "now," and all such deictic (that is, pointing) expressions deserve to be called "shifters" because the direction of their reference shifts according to the circumstances of their use—who utters or writes the words, where, and when.[15] "Here" and "now" are more shifty than most other shifters (e.g., "I" or "tomorrow") because not only their basic reference points but even their respective scope can radically change from one use to the next: "now" may refer to an instant or a decade, "here" may refer to a square inch or a whole country. "We" may in turn be the shiftiest of all shifters, since it is capable of invoking referents of radically different kinds in various combinations. It sometimes refers, as a well-behaved first-person plural pronoun always would, to people who utter "we" simultaneously or to people who have coauthored a text in which the word occurs. Yet, as discussed before, the referential range of "we" can be restricted to the speaker or writer alone, and it can also be extended to cover any number of second persons being addressed or any number of third persons being mentioned

15. A handy definition of deixis can be found in John Lyons, *Semantics* (Cambridge: Cambridge University Press, 1977), 2:636: "The term 'deixis' (which comes from a Greek word meaning 'pointing' or 'indicating') is now used in linguistics to refer to the function of personal and demonstrative pronouns, of tense and of a variety of other grammatical and lexical features which relate utterances to the spatio-temporal co-ordinates of the act of utterance." See also Charles J. Fillmore, *Santa Cruz Lectures on Deixis 1971* (Bloomington: Indiana University Linguistics Club, 1975). The helpful term "shifter" has been widely adopted from Roman Jakobson, "Shifters, Verbal Categories, and the Russian Verb" (1957), reprinted in *Selected Writings*, vol. 2 (The Hague: Mouton, 1971), pp. 130–47. The fountainhead of modern studies of *deixis* is, however, Part 2 of Karl Bühler's *Sprachtheorie* (note 25 to chapter 1), pp. 79–148 (pp. 91–166 in the English version).

while either including or excluding the actual sender of the verbal message. It goes almost without saying that such grammatical shiftiness must have rhetorical roots and consequences, to some of which we (my prospective readers and I) will now (at this point in my writing and their reading) turn.

## The Rhetoric of Saying "We"

A change in approach is called for as we proceed from considering grammatical options to considering rhetorical situations. It is one thing to observe that the author of a book written in a particular language (e.g., modern English)[16] *may* refer to himself or herself either as "I" or as "we." It is an altogether different thing to examine the intended or likely effect of the author's actual pronoun choice in a particular communicative situation. The latter kind of examination should consider the message sender's communicative intentions, the addressees' willingness to honor or at least recognize those intentions, the interlocutors' respective social standing, their ideological predilections, and many other factors. Furthermore, a thorough rhetorical analysis might well take into account how the rhetorical analyst's own motives, attitudes, and goals affect his or her interpretation of, say, Perot's, Clinton's, or Rorty's use of the pronoun "we" in particular acts of communication.

Focusing on particular communicative situations, the rhetorician needs to avoid turning plausible local findings into unwarranted global rules. For example, it is tempting to characterize the authorial "we" as a verbal means of self-aggrandizement even though its use can also stem from intended, unintended, or

---

16. Here I must ignore the thorny question of what a "particular language" is. The relevant subquestions include When does a language, in its historical development, undergo sufficient change to be regarded as having become a different language? and To what extent should some or all dialects count as different languages with partly overlapping grammars?

pretended self-effacement. Let me illustrate. In writing "we shall explore in the next chapter," a withdrawing author may be trying to adopt the perspective of the text; in writing "as we proceed," a neighborly author may wish to invite readers to share the inquiry. Now, the author's choice of "we" for either kind of attenuated self-reference can be challenged as, say, disingenuous or hegemonic. But it should be so challenged only if, in the rhetorical situation at hand, there is reason to suspect the sincerity or appropriateness of this or that particular author's implied claim of having abandoned his or her author-itarian stance. Likewise, the royal plural in "We grieve the death of your brave son" may sometimes be appreciated as a proper expression of nationwide sympathy even though a ruler's claim to speak on behalf of a whole country is frequently self-serving or otherwise doubtful.

Doing rhetorical justice to some instances of what I called the custodial use of "we" can be especially tricky. For example, the butler's avoidance of direct address in "Are we dining out tonight?" will typically signal his subservient identification with his employer's perspective. But the same question might be put antagonistically by a sarcastic parent to a spendthrift son or daughter. The doctor's question, "How are we feeling today?" will often be felt to diminish the patient's personal autonomy, yet the same question sometimes expresses empathic identification. Clearly enough, a large number of factors including the speaker's tone of voice and the addressee's social standing (welfare patient or head of state, to evoke extreme cases) should be considered in a rhetorically sensitive analysis of the doctor's utterance. After all, a doctor or nurse may have a range of different conscious and unconscious motives for not establishing pronominal distance between the sender and the receiver of the inquiry by asking, perhaps, "Well, Mr. Smith, will you tell me how you are feeling today?" Likewise, the adoptive grammar of "Aren't we cute?" calls for different rhetorical analyses when an adoring parent speaks the words about his or

her toddler and when the same question is uttered in the bar-
bershop about a *Playboy* centerfold.[17]

The last example shows "we" at its reifying worst, or just
about. But even such typical and apparently harmless utterances
as "We are older than you" or "We must keep this a secret" may
be felt by a person included in the "we"-reference as preemptive
of his or her right to reject the inclusion. Furthermore, it is rhetorically significant that some exclusion from the "we" group cannot
help but occur through the very use of this seemingly so cordial
pronoun. The so-called exclusive use of "we" in "We are older
than you" pits *our* side against *yours*, while its so-called limited
inclusive use in "We should keep this a secret" pits *our* side
against *theirs*.[18] And should an instance of "we" include all past,
present, and future human beings (e.g., "We are neither beasts
nor angels"), it still presupposes the existence of some "them"
(e.g., beasts and angels) who may sometimes be addressed as
"you" but cannot become some of "us."

Occasional exceptions[19] notwithstanding, saying "we" typically confirms or establishes the existence of some human group

17. In some spoken, written, or mental uses of the adoptive "we," desire for
exploiting another person's body may merge with admiring identification with
it. Rhetorical analyses of such merging, especially in homosexual and bisexual
discourses, could but need not follow the Lacanian paths traveled by Diana
Fuss, "Fashion and the Homospectatorial Look," *Critical Inquiry* 18 (1992):
713–37.

18. Needless to say, the grammarian's technical terms "exclusive," "limited
inclusive," and "inclusive" can be quite misleading when applied to concrete
rhetorical situations. On the one hand, the supposedly exclusive "we" may include any number of people *other than* the addressee(s). On the other hand, the
typical scope of the so-called limited inclusive "we" is more limited than inclusive: it excludes everyone *except* the addressee(s) and addressee(s). Even the
presumably altogether inclusive use of "we," permitting the inclusion of any
number of addressed and unaddressed persons in a statement like "We have
built this country together," excludes many people (i.e. the inhabitants of other
countries).

19. For example, the title of Charles A. Lindbergh's book *We* (New York:
Grosset and Dunlap, 1927) includes the author's airplane in its range of reference. Likewise, pets and the personified animals of myths and fables are sometimes included among the referents of "we."

as such. The individuals belonging to the group may be enemies, as when I say about myself and another person that "we are locked in fierce battle." Much more frequently, however, saying "we" indicates the desired or actual presence of a community of mutual interest, respect, or love. This can be the case even if the speaker or writer of a sentence is not literally included in the reference of "we." Consider the three instances of the corporate "we" cited in the previous section: "We are missing too many free throws today," "We signed the peace treaty under duress," and "We should have a reliable cancer cure in a hundred years." Those sentences suggest that their respective senders and addressees share with the proper referents of the pronoun—the ballplayers, the signatories, future human generations—the communal identity of a fan club, a nation, or a cancer-prone species.[20]

In evoking communal participation, "we" can function, or appear to function, as a pronoun of solidarity. Its mutual use by several people is thus analogous to the reciprocal use of informal address (e.g., tu/tu in French, du/du in German, Jeff/Sue in English) rather than to their asymmetrical use (e.g., vous/tu, Sie/du, Dr. Smith/Sue).[21] In the shift from formal to informal address, the grammar of power differential is expected to give way to the grammar of reciprocal solidarity at the suggestion of the higher-ranking or presumably more respected person. Likewise, it may well behoove the advantaged party to play the rhetorical role of initiating the inclusion, favored by Rorty, of "more and more dif-

20. Much of the grammatical shiftiness of the corporate "we" may indeed be attributed to its rhetorical implication of a virtual community to which the senders and receivers of a message like "We are missing too many free throws today" figuratively belong. On such a view, most corporate, custodial, and adoptive uses of "we" are comparable to the initially figurative but eventually literalized use of so-called dead metaphors (e.g., "the foot of the mountain" or "dead metaphor").

21. See Roger Brown and Albert Gilman, "The Pronouns of Power and Solidarity," in *Style in Language*, ed. Thomas Sebeok (Cambridge: MIT Press, 1960), and Roger Brown and Marguerite Ford, "Address in American English," *Journal of Abnormal and Social Psychology* 62 (1961): 375–85.

ferent sorts of people" within the range of "us."[22] I hasten to add that those on the other side of the "deep social cleavages" noted by Fraser[23] need to receive more than mere grammatical tokens of solidarity. Their grammatical ability to say (and think and feel) "we" in particular languages should in principle lead to equal rhetorical opportunity to function as active first, receptive second, or represented third parties in any scene of communication.

## The Logic of Saying "We"

The simultaneous relevance of those three functions informs Karl Bühler's astute characterization of the linguistic sign (*Sprachzeichen*) as symptom, signal, and symbol: expression by sender, appeal to receiver, and representation of objects and states of affairs.[24] Virtually all languages project this triadic structure of communication into the first, second, and third persons of their grammar.[25] In English, for example, *I* and *you* (interchangeably active and receptive partners) converse about *him*,

22. Cf. Richard Rorty, "On Ethnocentrism: A Reply to Clifford Geertz," *Michigan Quarterly Review* 25 (1986): 530: "The formulation of general moral principles has been less useful for the development of liberal institutions than has the gradual expansion of the imagination of those in power, their gradual willingness to use the term 'we' to include more and more different sorts of people." Concerning the role of pronouns in child development, see Eve V. Clark, "From Gesture to Word: On the Natural History of Deixis in Language Acquisition," in *Human Growth and Development*, ed. Jerome S. Bruner and Alison Garton (London: Oxford University Press, 1978), and Dan R. Laks, Leila Beckwith, and Sarale E. Cohen, "Mothers' Use of Personal Pronouns When Talking with Toddlers," *Journal of Genetic Psychology* 151 (1990): 25–32.

23. See note 2 above.

24. See note 25 to chapter 1. Amplifying Bühler's model, Jürgen Habermas has associated the symptomatic, signaling, and symbolic functions of verbal communication with three different "worlds" in which the respective validity claims of subjective sincerity, intersubjective rightness, and objective truth can be adjudicated. See esp. Jürgen Habermas, *Theorie des kommunikativen Handelns*, vol. 1, *Handlungsrationalität und gesellschaftliche Rationalisierung* (1981), 3d rev. ed. (Frankfurt: Suhrkamp, 1985), pp. 372–76 et passim; English version (see note 2 to prologue), pp. 275–78 et passim.

25. For possible exceptions, see note 10 above.

*her, it,* and *them* (represented third parties in the ongoing communication process). From a culturalist vantage point it could even be argued that it is our communicative capacity for playing active, receptive, and represented roles in verbal exchanges that situates each of us at the very crossroads of personal identity, interpersonal activity, and impersonal facticity. But there is no need to decide whether language or thought—grammar's egg or logic's chicken—came first. Our constant oscillation between the roles of first, second, and third persons in verbal messages and our permanent self-insertion into the subjective, intersubjective, and objective dimensions of life may well be complementary aspects of human worlds—intertwined conditions and consequences of each other.

It is a remarkable feature of pronouns like "we" and "us" that in uttering, writing, or thinking them a person can combine any two or all three of the communicative perspectives of his or her lifeworld. When "we" refers only to the sender and the addressee(s) of a verbal message, its "limited inclusive" use integrates the first and at least one second person—me and you—into what might be called the interlocutors' *conspiratorial* "us." When "we" refers only to the sender and one or more members of the sender's (absent or at present silent) community, its so-called "exclusive" use integrates the first and one or more third persons—me and some of them—into what might be called the spokesperson's *adversarial* "us." Each of these two kinds of integration entails a complementary kind of segregation. The conspiratorial "us" unites me and you against them; the adversarial "us" unites me and those of them who are mine against you and those of them who are yours. More smoothly shifting inclusions and exclusions occur in certain cases discussed before: when, for instance, the speaker's or writer's "I" is submerged into an authorial or royal "we" or when a corporate, custodial, or adoptive "we" restricts its literal reference to one or more persons other than the speaker or writer. But "we" can also refer jointly to sender, addressee(s), and their combined communities. In a proclamation like "We must protect our environment," an *ecumenical* "we"—my last coinage in this chapter—integrates first, second, and third persons into a potentially all-inclusive human community. In so doing, the ecumenical "we" recombines the first-, second-, and third-person perspectives of communication just as a rapidly spinning top turns the three cardinal colors painted on it into the whitish hue of unrefracted light.

Dare I suggest that such dizzying integration of the perspectives of "I," "you," and "they" fuses our personal, social, and natural horizons of being toward, with, and of the world into a panorama of all Being? Better not. The prospect of making the fragmentary human condition whole by the magic of a single word—or by a set of different words used in some languages for inclusive or exclusive, dual, triple, or limitlessly plural equivalents[26] of the English "we"—can only be a dream, of course. Furthermore, rhetorical analysis often reveals that co-optive rather than cooperative motives and effects are associated with the grammatical expression of total solidarity. Yet the utopian logic of universal participation in the "we" of a diverse worldwide community allows *us*, whoever we are here and now, to engage in intelligent critiques of the local languages and situations from which, deplorably, a consistent global practice of communal identity has not yet emerged.

For the foreseeable future, most of our "we"-saying will remain fraught with complementary inclusions and exclusions among first, second, and third persons. Even so, the promise held out by the grammatical possibility of an ecumenical "we" should encourage us to prefer an as yet fragmented threefold pronominal horizon to the single undifferentiated perspective subserved by indefinite generic pronouns. Like French *on* and German *man*,

26. The fullest known range of such distinctions is illustrated from Fijian by Anderson and Keenan (see note 7 above), p. 263. In clear contrast, many languages share with English grammar its lack of formal concern as to the exact number of plural referents—whether "we" are just the two or three or more of "us."

English "one" usually includes the sender and the addressee of a message in its range of blurred reference but requires the ensuing verb to appear in the third-person singular. In other words, indefinite generic pronouns tend to reduce what you and I can do to what "one does," thereby turning us, interactive participants in life and communication, into inert referents of other people's discourse.[27] Such a reified view of human beings has indeed been ascribed by Martin Heidegger to the inauthentic mentality of *das Man*—his personification of the German generic pronoun with the neuter gender added.[28] It appears, however, that our recalcitrant tribe of interactive first and second persons manages to hold its own as we continue to make capacious use of a variety of personal pronouns (in English, "you," "we," and "they") in contexts where grammar would allow us to slip into the depersonalized language of "one," *man*, *on*, and other generic pronouns.[29]

27. I don't mean to suggest that persons spoken of in the third grammatical person are always treated in an *impersonal* way. But their status as third persons in a communicative act does place them, at least for the time being, outside the shared *interpersonal* realm within which first and second persons can intervene in each other's *personal* lives.

28. The gender implication is lost in the English rendering of *das Man* as "the 'They' "; see Martin Heidegger, *Sein und Zeit* (Halle: Niemeyer, 1927), pp. 126–30; English version: *Being and Time*, trans. John MacQuarrie and Edward Robinson (New York: Harper, 1962), pp. 163–68. To be sure, grammar does not amount to rhetorical or logical destiny: the alienated, "average" mentality of *das Man* is often manifested by "we"-sayers and, conversely, not every occurrence of a generic pronoun will attest to a reified view of human agency. The French indefinite pronoun has even found at least one enthusiastic defender in Monique Wittig, a leading voice in current lesbian feminist theory and fiction. Even though *on* ("one") is typically followed by the masculine form of adjectives and past participles associated with it, Wittig accepts what "the grammarians say" about such masculine forms being "in fact neuter." Accordingly, she finds that *on* is "neither gendered nor numbered" and thus "lends itself to the unique experience of all locutors who, when saying it, can reappropriate the whole language and reorganize the world from their point of view." See Wittig's "The Mark of Gender," in *The Poetics of Gender*, ed. Nancy K. Miller (New York: Columbia University Press, 1966), pp. 68–69.

29. Recent discussions of the use of personal in lieu of impersonal pronouns include M. Stanley Whitley, "Person and Number in the Use of *We, You,* and *They,*" *American Speech* 53 (1978): 18–39; Dwight Bolinger, "To Catch a Metaphor: *You* as Norm," *American Speech* 54 (1979): 194–209; Roberta D. Gates,

Another kind of linguistic leveling is attempted through the monological idiom of "exact science," whose streamlined but necessarily narrow logic has been largely purified of the shifting rhetorical perspectives expressed in the three grammatical persons. Having suppressed or trying to conceal their own personal and social concerns, some proponents of impersonal logic appear eager to disregard or eliminate deixis, which is grammar's primary means of reflecting the rhetorical anchoring of all discourse in particular acts of communication.[30] I have no fear that "their" kind of discourse might prevail over "ours" because they are, really, some of us. Even if the mathematically based sciences continued to have virtually no use for deictic terms and concepts like "I" and "here" and "now," the lifeworlds that scientific experts share with other people would remain relative to those readily shifting, but temporarily always fixed, points of dialogical orientation. I doubt, for instance, whether an astronomer can study the evidence for and against the existence of black holes without occasionally pondering just how far they are from those of us thinking about them here and now. Also, my geologist and historian colleagues subjectively expect to receive their paychecks on the same first working day of every month—an intersubjectively defined unit of our society's shared public time—despite the vastly different objective time scales of their disciplines. In any event, all expert languages need to be acquired and validated through ordinary verbal discourse whose pronominal system forcefully

"Broad Reference of Pronouns in Current Usage," *American Speech* 55 (1980): 228–31; and William J. Ashby, "The Variable Use of *On* versus *Tu/Vous* for Indefinite Reference in Spoken French," *Journal of French Language Studies* 2 (1992): 135–57. A remarkable correspondence has been observed in the spoken French of Montreal between the increasing use of *on* ("one") in the traditional sense of *nous* ("we") and the increasing use of *tu* and *vous* ("you") in the traditional sense of *on* ("one"); see Suzanne Laberge and Gillian Sankoff, "Anything *You* Can Do," in Gillian Sankoff, *The Social Use of Language* (Philadelphia: University of Pennsylvania Press, 1980).

30. Bühler (note 25 to chapter 1), pp. 366–85, already had much to say about the necessarily limited success of such an endeavor; pp. 418–37 in the English edition.

suggests that *we* can—and should—keep adding perspectival depth to the flat vision of each specialized monocular *I*.

That suggestion has begun to be heeded with a vengeance in holistic reconceptions of the environment according to one of which "the conjoined life of the earth behaves like a huge, coherent, self-regulating organism."[31] If human survival depends on our positive or negative impact on the survival of organisms whose existence helps maintain the current temperature and chemical constitution of the atmosphere, there is indeed reason to extend the range of "we" beyond the frontiers of the human species. And there is equally good or even better reason for at least some physical and biological sciences to adjust their grammar and rhetoric to the logic of what their own theory and practice reveal about the interactive emergence and shifting configurations of observers and phenomena.

As a matter of fact, every human *I* is one such interactive configuration: an observingly observed "society of mind"[32] rather than some Cyclopean mental eye fixed, once and for all, in the dead center of an otherwise mindless body. When the configurative process of always becoming—never being—a complete self functions well, the *I* interacts with all it becomes conscious of while experiencing itself as becoming conscious of becoming conscious. This self-making process, whose social dimension will be explored further in the next chapter, may be described in modified Freudian terms as follows. Each of us applies first-, third-, and sec-

31. Lewis Thomas, *The Fragile Species* (New York: Scribner, 1992), p. 120. Influenced by James E. Lovelock and Lynn Margulis, the two scientists principally associated with the Gaia hypothesis, Thomas repeatedly commented on the interrelatedness of all life on the earth in short essays first published in the *New England Journal of Medicine* and later gathered into *The Lives of a Cell: Notes of a Biology Watcher* (New York: Viking, 1974). For a recent restatement of the hypothesis and a brief review of the pertinent literature, see Margulis and Lovelock, "Gaia and Geognosy," in *Global Ecology: Towards a Science of the Biosphere*, ed. Mitchell B. Rambler et al. (San Diego: Academic Press, 1989).

32. I borrow this phrase from the title of Marvin Minsky, *The Society of Mind* (New York: Simon and Schuster, 1986), without subscribing to all of Minsky's ideas and arguments.

ond-person perspectives as we embody our conscious I (*Ich*), abide the world of Them including the unconscious It (*Es*), and converse with the internalized voices of significant others so that their plural You is kept from rigidifying into an alien, depersonalized superego or Above-I (*Überich*). In other words, the internal process of unfinishable selfing replicates within each person the external processes of ongoing interpersonal communication. Just as our interaction with other selves, role-players, and organisms sometimes succeeds in fusing the first-, second-, and third-person aspects of being human into a composite "we"-perspective of communal identity, so too the personal, social, and biological dimensions of the psyche can overcome the danger of schizophrenic separation and become fused in an individual's three-dimensional being toward, with, and of the world. In our most felicitous moments, we thus catch a glimpse of who *we* are: occasional realizations of a potential, manifested in language, that can bring unity into the diversity—and diversity into the unity—of culture, existence, and experience.

# Chapter Four

## Society, Nature, Selves: Freedom and Diversity

In the preceding chapter I explored some of the ways a composite "we"-perspective informs, and may be enlisted to transform, human worlds. This chapter's related task is to suggest how the radical intertwining of social, natural, and individual strains in all being and becoming informs, and may be enlisted to transform, human freedom and diversity.

### Four Principles of Being and Becoming

The intertwining is radical because it occurs from the root up. Ever since the beginning, nature has been plural: *it* exists as a multiplicity of *them*. But the creative Big Bang gave rise to force fields of mutual impact rather than isolated entities. Thus the principle of society (the Many as One) manifested itself right along with the principle of nature (the One as Many). Individuality, in the human sense of self-aware personal identity, came much later. But its principle (the One as One) was evident already at the bangy beginning: without one(s), no many. Indeed, nature, society, and individuality have always been in each other's company while a fourth principle—the Many as Many—keeps sustaining the differences among them. This fourth principle—the principle of diversity—prompts most people in most cultures (if not indeed all people in all cultures) to experience the natural, social, and individual dimensions of their lives as interdependently autonomous.

The foregoing characterization of nature, society, individuality, and diversity harks back to Plato's *Parmenides*—a puzzling dialogue about the existence or nonexistence of the one and the many. Few arguments presented in that intriguingly inconclusive text remain as unqualified by direct reply or the general context as the following statement made by Parmenides: "Every thing in relation to every other thing is either the same or other; or if neither the same nor other, then in the relation of a part to a whole, or of a whole to a part" (146 in Jowett's translation). I feel justified in unpacking the sentence just quoted as follows. Four principles cooperate in all being and becoming: the One as Many underlies the articulation of wholes into parts, the Many as One underlies the integration of parts into wholes, the One as One underlies identity or sameness, and the Many as Many underlies difference or otherness. My variation on the ancient theme aligns the respective principles of articulation, integration, sameness, and otherness with the *natural, social,* and *individual* ways of all things always being, and ever becoming differently, *diverse.*

In the realm of physics, concepts like gravitation and electromagnetism help us grasp how the principle of integration could pervade the pluriverse even before the emergence of life greatly enhanced the scope of sociality in it. Moving from inorganic to organic chemistry, we face ever more intricate concatenations of disparate ingredients, and microbiology tells us that every living cell integrates contrary capacities: its proteins metabolize other substances while its nucleic acids (DNA and RNA) replicate themselves.[1] Larger-scale forms of togetherness known as symbiosis also abound in the ever evolving domain of life.[2] Most symbiotic relationships are functional rather than structural, as is the case with the indispensable biological assistance we humans receive from microbes living in our breathing and digestive systems. But some participants in symbiotic cooperation eventually give up their existence as members of separate species. For example, the mitochondria of today—ubiquitous organelles exploiting oxygen as an energy source in the cells of plants and animals—seem to have evolved from free-living rod-shaped bacteria.[3] Clearly, no One is a biological island in the sea of Many. All organisms depend on their environment for survival, and in the countless plant and animal species relying on sexual reproduction, each new living individual presupposes something like the combinatory union of parental sperm and egg.

## The Grammar and Rhetoric of Self-Making

It is tempting to think that we humans are somehow more individual than members of other species. But if we are, we surely owe the privilege to our being more social as well. After

1. As far as I can tell, the dual nature of full-fledged life is not in serious dispute. Freeman J. Dyson, *Infinite in All Directions* (New York: Harper and Row, 1988), even postulates the likelihood of a dual *origin* of life: "The first protein creatures might have existed independently for a long time, eating and growing and gradually evolving a more and more efficient metabolic apparatus. The nucleic acid creatures must have been obligatory parasites from the start, preying upon the protein creatures and using the products of protein metabolism to achieve their own replication" (p. 64). Stephen Jay Gould, realizing that Dyson's hypothesis has not yet been vindicated, is not alone among scientists and others in "rooting for him." See Gould's review of Dyson's book in the *New York Review of Books*, October 27, 1988, pp. 32–34.
2. The title essay in Lewis Thomas, *The Medusa and the Snail* (New York: Viking, 1979), interconnects notions of selfhood and symbiosis. Thomas also makes interesting remarks on "societies as organisms" in *The Lives of a Cell* (note 31 to chapter 3), pp. 11–15 et passim.
3. Cf. Lynn Margulis and Dorion Sagan, *Microcosm: Four Billion Years of Evolution from Our Microbial Ancestors* (New York: Summit, 1986), pp. 128–33.

all, the human infant's very "premature" birth necessitates an exceptionally long period of parental and societal care.[4] During that period the infant begins to perceive itself in the mirror of other people's reactions.[5] Since many of the reactions in question are verbally expressed, the child must acquire grammatical and rhetorical competence to take full advantage of society's mirrors.[6]

Acculturation to the pronoun system of a language plays a particularly important role in the development of our sense of both identity and community. On the one hand, the growing child learns to adopt the subject position of an *I*-saying person toward a world of verbally interactive *you*s and (at the moment) noncommunicative *they*s. On the other hand, the child also learns the grammatical and rhetorical habits of extending personal identity through the temporary inclusion of other persons and personalized nonhumans in the shifting referential range of *we*. As a result, the rhetorical perspectives of first, second, and third grammatical persons—our horizons of being toward, with, and of the world— are acquired together with the composite "we"-perspective—a

---

4. See, for instance, David Jonas and Doris Klein, *Man-Child: The Infantilization of Man* (New York: McGraw-Hill, 1970).

5. Such a "looking-glass self," so called by the American social psychologist Charles Horton Cooley as early as 1902, begins to form long before most infants regularly encounter their optical image in actual mirrors. More recently, Anselm L. Strauss and D. W. Winnicott used the mirror metaphor in their respective explorations of personal identity. Jacques Lacan in turn stressed the self-shaping role of actual mirrors in the psychological development of infants. See Charles Horton Cooley, *Human Nature and the Social Order* (New York: Scribner, 1902), p. 152; Anselm L. Strauss, *Mirrors and Masks: The Search for Identity* (Glencoe, Ill.: Free Press, 1959); D. W. Winnicott, "The Mirror Role of Mother and Family in Child Development" (1967), in his *Playing and Reality* (London: Tavistock, 1971), pp. 111–18; Jacques Lacan, "The Mirror Stage as Formative of the Function of the I as Revealed in Psychoanalytic Experience" (1949), in his *Ecrits: A Selection*, trans. Alan Sheridan (London: Tavistock, 1977), pp. 1–7.

6. Rudimentary instances of such mirroring have been observed in prelingual infants and some higher animals. Yet full-fledged human minds, societies, and even brains cannot evolve without the acquisition of a specifically human set of utterable or, as among deaf people, gesturable means of representation, communication, and expression.

fourth mode of mental vision in which the other three interface in diverse combinations.[7] The self's evolution in the collective womb of society is at least as complex and puzzling as the course of embryonic development proper. The initial formation of a psychological mother/child dyad typically precedes the offspring's assumption of personhood with its own center of mental gravity.[8] Soon enough, however, the "biologic individual" becomes a "self" through what George H. Mead has described as the "importation of the social process" (p. 186).[9] Self-consciousness, according to Mead, is "the awakening in ourselves of the group of attitudes which we are arousing in others" (p. 163). The awakening of such transposed attitudes is greatly aided by verbal utterances, because "vocal gestures" (unlike facial expressions, for example) can be simultaneously per-

7. See Rom Harré, "The Self in Monodrama," in *The Self: Psychological and Philosophical Issues*, ed. Theodore Mischel (Oxford: Blackwell, 1977), esp. pp. 340–41: "Personal pronouns are not learned as referential atomic names, but rather as a system, for which mutuality of person recognition is a necessary condition." Harré and I differ in our respective assessments of the "we"-perspective, which he joins Erving Goffman in assimilating to the second-person perspective of "you." For example, Harré writes: "Human beings from a very early age form 'we's,' Goffmanian 'withs,' and social life develops within a given intersubjectivity." In my scheme of things, any "given" intersubjectivity remains in the second-person domain of a role-player's "being with" one, or more than one, particular "you." By contrast, and for reasons explored in the previous chapter, a truly distinctive "we" perspective fuses at least two of our three horizons of being with, being of, and being toward the world.

8. See Rom Harré, *Social Being: A Theory for Social Psychology* (Totowa, N.J.: Rowman and Littlefield, 1980), pp. 329–31, and several papers included in *The Integration of a Child into a Social World*, ed. Martin P. M. Richards (Cambridge: Cambridge University Press, 1974). Most "motherly" functions can, of course, be carried out by primary caregivers of either gender. Therefore psychological dyads other than actual mother-child relations, as well as quasi-Oedipal triads of various sorts, will also be formed.

9. See George H. Mead, *Mind, Self, and Society from the Standpoint of a Social Behaviorist* (Chicago, 1934), part 3, "The Self" (pp. 135–226), as well as two supplementary essays, "The Biologic Individual" (pp. 347–53) and "The Self and the Process of Reflection" (pp. 354–78). Ruth Leys, "Mead's Voices: Imitation as Foundation, or, The Struggle against Mimesis," *Critical Inquiry* 19 (winter 1993): 277–307, provides useful information both about Mead's intellectual roots and about the reception of his work.

ceived, interpreted, and acted upon by selves and others—utterers and hearers—alike (pp. 358–69). As the internalized attitudes of individual others merge in the developing mind of a child or prehistoric adult into the attitude of what Mead has termed the "generalized other," his or her *me* constitutes itself in relation to what others, generally, expect it to be (pp. 154–59).

The emergence of such a *me* is, however, not the entire story. Mead contrasts the *me* to the *I* as "two phases of the self" (p. 192). They are, roughly, the object and the subject of self-consciousness but also, and more interestingly, the socially scripted and the individually improvised dimension of a person's behavior (pp. 173–78). Mead insists on the constant internal "give-and-take" between the two phases that jointly "constitute the personality": "There would not be an 'I' in the sense in which we use that term if there were not a 'me'; there would not be a 'me' without a response in the form of the 'I' " (p. 182). By responsively interpreting and even adopting the generalized other's attitude toward *me*, my *I* outgrows what used to be the organism's unself-conscious center of bodily awareness.[10] Having turned into a reflective agent, such an *I* even becomes capable of comprehending "the voices of the past and of the future" and thus of "setting up a higher sort of community which in a sense out-votes the one we find" (pp. 167 f.).[11]

10. Mead says rightly, I believe, that "the taking or feeling of the attitude of the other toward yourself is what constitutes self-consciousness, and not the mere organic sensations of which the individual is aware and which he experiences" (pp. 171–72). But precisely because self-consciousness results from the "taking" and even "feeling" of an "attitude" toward—rather than from the acquisition of some knowledge or belief about—oneself, I wish Mead had refrained from insisting, against the views of William James and Charles Cooley, that "the essence of the self . . . is cognitive" rather than "affective experience with its motor accompaniments" (p. 173). As I suggest in the next chapter, feelings, beliefs, and desires (as well as socially shared attitudes, worldviews, and projects) are intertwined in self-consciousness.

11. Mead says that a person who is "going against the whole world about him" must "speak with the voice of reason to himself." In the context of Mead's pertinent views, this should be understood in nonabsolutist terms: one speaks with "the voice of reason" only in ways that are available in the particular social world against which the person in question aspires to "stand out by

The double lesson of Mead's explorations can therefore be phrased as follows. On the one hand, *natural* human organisms reach ever higher levels of *personal* awareness as they internalize some of their lifelong "conversation of significant gestures" (p. 192) with other members of their *society*. On the other hand, *socially* constructed *persons* can push the *natural* evolution of the human species ever further by refusing to accept wholesale any currently dominant "community standards" (p. 168).[12] Nature, society, and individuality[13] thus cooperate to effect change in each of their diverse but intertwined dimensions.

In some ways Mead's description of the emergence of the self amplifies Martin Buber's meditations on the language-based entanglement of every self with its social and natural others. In *I and Thou*, first published in German in 1923 but probably unknown to Mead, Buber wrote: "There is no *I* taken in itself, but only the *I* of the primary word *I-Thou* and the *I* of the primary word *I-It*. When a man says *I* he refers to one or the other of these. . . . Further, when he says *Thou* or *It*, the *I* of one of the two primary words is present."[14]

himself" (p. 68). In other words, Mead's "I" is not a disembodied transcendental ego communing with other purely rational beings but, rather, a biological individual's *natural* awareness *personalized* through *social* interaction.

12. In the helpful terms coined by Raymond Williams, individual "structures of feeling" often pit "preemergent" cultural patterns against the "residual," dominant," or "emergent" aspects of a shared ideology. See his *Marxism and Literature* (London: Oxford University Press, 1977), pp. 121–35.

13. Individuality, as one of four interactive principles of being and becoming, should not be confused with any of the different kinds of individual*ism* critically surveyed in Steven Lukes, *Individualism* (Oxford: Blackwell, 1973); cf. also C. B. MacPherson, *The Political Theory of Possessive Individualism: Hobbes to Locke* (Oxford: Clarendon, 1962).

14. Martin Buber, *Ich und Du* (1923; Berlin: Schocken, 1936), p. 10. Quoted from *I and Thou*, trans. Ronald Gregor Smith, 2d ed. (New York: Scribner, 1958), p. 4. "Primary word" is Smith's English rendering of *Grundwort*. While calling Buber's book "untranslatable," Walter Kaufmann nonetheless attempted his own annotated translation of *I and Thou* (New York: Scribner, 1970). Kaufmann retained the earlier translator's title but changed "thou" to "you" in the text because "the recurrent 'Thou' in the first translation mesmerized people to the point where it was widely assumed that Buber was a theologian," even though Buber's book, on Kaufmann's reading, "deals centrally with man's relationships to other men" (p. 38).

In Buber's view, "primary words do not describe something that might exist independently of them, but being spoken they bring about existence" (p. 3). This applies to both primary words *I-Thou* and *I-It*, but the creative power of each is different because *I-Thou* emerged before, and *I-It* emerged after, "primitive man . . . recognized himself as *I*" (p. 22). Buber continues:

The first primary word can be resolved, certainly, into *I* and *Thou*, but it did not arise from their being set together; by its nature, it precedes *I*. The second word arose from the setting together of *I* and *It*: by nature it comes after *I*. . . . Whenever the sentence "I see the tree" is so uttered that it no longer tells of a relation between the man—*I*—and the tree—*Thou*—, but establishes the perception of the tree as object by the human consciousness, the barrier between subject and object has been set up. The primary word *I-It*, the word of separation, has been spoken. (pp. 22–23)[15]

Much of what the religious thinker Buber proclaims about the spiritual primacy of *I-Thou* relations is echoed in a different conceptual register when the social theorist Mead says:

The self is not something that exists first and then enters into relationship with others, but it is, so to speak, an eddy in the social current and so still a part of the current. . . . The physical object is an abstraction which we make from the social response to nature. We talk to nature; we address the clouds, the sea, the tree, and objects about us. We later abstract from that type of response because of what we come to know about such objects. The immediate response is, however, social. (pp. 182, 184)

Taken together, Buber's and Mead's views about the emergence of selves suggest the following account of cosmic chronology. Interlinked particulars presumably existed of and with the

15. The German text cited in the previous note contrasts the two primary words as *vorichhaft* and *nachichhaft* (p. 30) and distinguishes between *Baum-Du* and *Baum-Gegenstand* with respect to trees (p. 31).

world before the dawning of personal identity enabled some of them to position themselves toward it. Yet the natural domain of *Its* (to be individuated as such by one of Buber's two *I*s) and the social domain of Buber's *I-Thou* relations would not be what they are without self-conscious individuals who are able to pick out themselves as Meadian *Me*s and other particulars as *Its* or *Thou*s from what thereby becomes some one's natural and social environment.[16]

Now, Mead's distinction between *I* and *Me* is based on how grammatical case indicates the sender's position as either the subject or the object of an instance of spoken, written, or mental discourse. Buber's distinctions between *I*, *Thou*, and *It* in turn draw on the grammatical projections of the respective functions of senders, addressees, and represented referents in verbal communication. Having to do with shifting positions and alternating functions, the pronominal distinctions invoked by Mead and Buber are rhetorical in origin. The reason they have become grammaticalized in the case and person systems of virtually all languages may well be that both sets of distinctions are indispensable to effective verbal communication.[17]

Needless to say, participants in verbal interactions mentally make many additional distinctions as well—for example, distinc-

16. The future possibility of conscious towardness could even be regarded as the retroactive guarantor of individuality. See, for instance, Stephen R. L. Clark, "Aware If Alive," *TLS* (August 6, 1993): 28: "Until there are conscious beings, indeed, there is no reason to identify singular individuals within a distinct environment. Till then there is only biochemical process, without any privileged viewpoints: why think of an acorn as an entity, rather than as part of a gene's environment? Why think of 'the gene' as an entity within an environment?" I am sympathetic to the sentiment Clark expresses in this review of Raymond Tallis, *The Explicit Animal: A Defence of Human Consciousness* (note 27 to chapter 1), but I would add that the "privileged viewpoint" of a conscious being is less the viewpoint of an "entity" than it is the shifting vantage point of a process of selfing.

17. No case markers or lexically distinct forms are necessary, of course, to express the positional and perspectival differences in question; in some languages, word order or verbal inflections can achieve the same grammatical purpose.

tions concerning the gender and social standing of the speaker or writer, listener(s) or reader(s), and other mentioned person(s). Since no language supplies grammatically distinct means to express all possible distinctions of this kind, people must fine-tune their sense of socially embedded selfhood by availing themselves of circumlocution, figures of speech, and other rhetorical vehicles of communication.[18] For example, it is by no means necessary to acquire competence in such an elaborate system of grammatical cases as the Latin nominative, accusative, genitive, dative, ablative, and vocative in order to "learn" to be subjects, objects, possessors, recipients, instruments, and partners in cultural transactions. Conversely, Hungarian children do not seem to develop a particularly positive or negative attitude toward sexuality just because the pronoun system of their native tongue fails to make third-person gender distinctions corresponding to "he" and "she" in English. In short, it is not only through grammar— the relatively fixed system of cases, pronouns, and the like in a particular language —that the growing child turns relationships with others into a personal sense of situated identity. At least to the same extent, we become selves among selves through our constant rhetorical performance of relatively malleable roles in particular communicative situations.

## Role-Playing, Responsibility, History

A person's self is far from being a monolith, of course. Just as every organism, while alive, must keep in approximate balance the reciprocal contributions of its various parts to their combined well-being, so every person or self, while operative as such, must keep

18. It has long been observed that every language can indirectly express through circumlocution whatever another language directly expresses through grammatical means. Languages therefore differ in what they must (rather than what they can) convey; see Roman Jakobson, "On Linguistic Aspects of Translation" (1959), reprinted in *Selected Writings*, vol. 2, *Word and Language* (The Hague: Mouton, 1971), pp. 260–71, esp. p. 264.

in approximate balance the reciprocal contributions of *its* various parts. But what are the parts of individual selves? Proposals for subdividing the psyche into a handful of components have abounded ever since Plato offered his parable of the rational chari-oteer guiding two winged horses—one nobly spirited, the other enthralled to appetites (*Phaedrus* 246 and 253–54). William James, for example, divided the "constituents of the Self" into four classes: the material self, the social self, the spiritual self, and the pure ego.[19] Sigmund Freud in turn described the psyche as consisting of a drive-driven id, a largely self-conscious ego, and a socially im-posed superego.[20] Our frequent experience of great internal diver-sity hardly tallies with such broad typologies of mental life. Even in the mirrors of society, each of us appears to have more than just three or four different faces. "A man," observed William James himself, "has as many different social selves as there are distinct *groups* of persons about whose opinion he cares" (1:294).

Since each such group expects us to behave differently, I take James's statement to suggest that a particular person's most salient parts are indeed "parts"—socially ascribed roles that he or she feels called upon to perform in the course of a lifetime. For ex-ample, the *me* of a certain man—roughly outlined by his taking the attitude of the generalized other toward himself—becomes amplified through his being primarily regarded by different groups of people as a district attorney, a school board president, a member of the navy reserve, a father, a son, an ex-husband, and so forth. In playing the parts just mentioned, as well as numerous others, the man's *me* must stay fairly close to social scripts, but his *I* may occasionally improvise. Such improvising will alter the role that is being played; it can even modify society's conception of the role before it gets assigned to the *me* of another player. Fur-thermore, we play our various social roles with the alternating

19. William James, *The Principles of Psychology* (note 3 to Prologue), 1:292.
20. See esp. his "Das Ich und das Es," in *Gesammelte Werke* (London: Imago, 1940), 13:237–89. English version: "The Ego and the Id," in *The Standard Edition* (note 16 to chapter 1), 19 (1961): 1–66.

kinds and degrees of empathy that are required of performing artists—say, of an actress playing Hedda Gabler one night and Lady Macbeth the next—in a repertory theater. Indeed, our district attorney, school board president, and ex-husband (etc.) will vary the kinds and degrees of his personal identification with his various roles not only during public "performances" but also during the periods of private contemplation when he recalls or anticipates playing a particular part.

Contemplative recalling and imaginative anticipating are essential for every role-player's sense of having a personal history. Memory assigns responsibility for our autobiographical past, and imagination allows us to choose among possible future courses of action. Small wonder that some roles a person vividly remembers having played in the past or expectantly imagines playing in the future should have greater impact on his or her sense of selfhood than many currently executed social routines. Although the three Kantian "mental capacities"[21] enable us to know, will, and feel pleasure or displeasure in the ever fleeting present, it is through our conscience-laden memory and option-packed imagination that a human organism's biological processes assume the shape of a personal history within an evolving social lifeworld.

Much more will be said in the next chapter about the personal and social implications of knowing, willing, and feeling. I only wish to stress now that memory and imagination—the directedness of belief and desire toward a postulated past or a hypothetical future—affect not only the individual who does the remembering or imagining in question. Beyond any doubt, societal judgments and predictions heavily bear on one's own assessments and projections as to one's own past and future. In particular, mutual awareness that two or more persons share certain memories often leads to reciprocally constitutive impact on the ongoing formation

21. *Erkenntnisvermögen, Begehrungsvermögen,* and *Gefühle der Lust und Unlust*—see the second introduction, titled "On the Division of Philosophy," to Kant's *Critique of Judgment;* a pertinent passage is cited below (see note 12 to chapter 5).

of each separate self.[22] Likewise, knowingly shared expectations as to the imagined outcome of common projects can mutually shape the personal development of several people, especially when what they expect *of* each other is at issue.[23] To be sure, all remembering of the past is motivated by present circumstances and future goals, and all future projects reflect the past's impact on the projector's present situation. As a result our remembered past, experienced present, and projected future are not so much separate segments of an irreversible chronology as intertwined branches of recollection, attention, and imagination.[24] All the same, our twin

22. Thomas Luckmann has usefully extended the concept of "reciprocal mirroring" as an "elementary condition for the formation of personal identities" to cover the "mutual recollection of actions of the other in past face-to-face situations and the reciprocal imposition of responsibility for past actions." See his "Personal Identity as an Evolutionary and Historical Problem," in *Human Ethology: Claims and Limits of a New Discipline*, ed. M. von Cranach, K. Foppa, W. Lepenies, and D. Ploog, ed. (Cambridge: Cambridge University Press, 1979), p. 66. See also Alvin W. Gouldner, "The Norm of Reciprocity: A Preliminary Statement," *American Sociological Review* 25 (1960): 161–78, and David Middleton and Derek Edwards, eds. *Collective Remembering* (London: Sage, 1990).

23. Concerning the difference between *expecting of* and *expecting that*, see Stephen E. Toulmin, "Self Knowledge and Knowledge of the 'Self,'" in *The Self: Psychological and Philosophical Issues*, ed. Theodore Mischel (Oxford: Blackwell, 1977), esp. pp. 293–94: "The child comes to recognize what he can expect of other human beings; and this 'expecting of' goes far beyond any simple predictive 'expecting that' they will behave in one way rather than another." According to Toulmin, children's "communicative exchanges and joint activities with family and friends" give them "knowledge of persons" rather than "knowledge of phenomena" and eventually lead to the kind of "self-knowledge" that is "a product both of self-study and of self-creation" for the following reason: "The question, 'What should I expect of myself?', is not a narrowly cognitive or intellectual (i.e., predictive) question: it is an affective-volitional question, to be paraphrased as, 'What should I *hope for* and / or *demand of* myself?'"

24. Since every perceived *now* is shadowed by past and future *thens* and vice versa, our "specious present" is never restricted to a single experienced moment. As William James put it, "The practically cognized present is no knife-edge, but a saddle-back, with a certain breadth of its own on which we sit perched and from which we look in two directions into time." *The Principles of Psychology* (see note 3 to Prologue), 1:609. The term "specious present" was popularized by James. But the difficulties involved with any atomistic view of time have plagued philosophers ever since Zeno presented his famous paradox about the series of presumably distinct locations occupied by a continuously moving arrow.

capacity for recollecting and imagining—for looking backward into an already "closed" past and looking forward into an as yet "open" future—gives rise to our twin senses of responsibility and freedom.

It is of course far from clear just how free and responsible the individual players of biologically imposed or socially assigned roles really are. Lewis White Beck helpfully names and interrelates four concepts emerging from philosophical discussions of human self-determination as follows: the *agent* is free to act for justified reasons; the *actor* is determined by causes; the *spectator* believes others to be actors; and the *critic* is "in a position to agree" either with the agent that the agent is indeed a free agent or with the spectator that the would-be agent is in fact an unfree actor.[25] I hardly need to point out that listing such alternatives elicits rather than resolves the following questions: Can anyone choose to be an agent, actor, spectator, or critic, and if so, is the choosing (and thus chosen) self responsible for that choice? Can an actor, performing biologically imposed or socially assigned roles, discard those masks and astonish the spectator by revealing a free agent's usually concealed face?

Erving Goffman, perhaps the best-known theorist of social role-playing, seems to have denied the cogency of the very distinction between masks and faces when he wrote: "Just as the current situation prescribes the official guise behind which we will conceal ourselves, so it provides for where and how we will show through, the culture itself prescribing what sort of entity we must believe ourselves to be in order to have something to show through in this manner."[26] In Mead's terms one might say that for Goffman the *I* is a series of *me*s, all the way down. Consistently enough, Goffman's books do not attempt to explore who we are

25. Lewis White Beck, "Agent, Actor, Spectator, and Critic," *Monist* 49 (1965): 168.

26. Erving Goffman, *Frame Analysis* (Cambridge: Harvard University Press, 1974), p. 573.

or may become.[27] Rather, he aims at describing how individuals in social interactions discharge such functions as "figure," "animator," "strategist," and "principal."[28] In the context of a professional ball game, for example, the four partly overlapping functions would be assigned as follows: the coaches function as "strategists," the players serve as the "animators" of the "figures" that happen to be their own bodies, and the club owners and fans reap sufficient financial or emotional benefit to count as "principals." Another illustration, largely derived from Goffman, will make it plain that at least three of the four functions need not be tied to human agency. The typically nonhuman "figures" of a chess game are occasionally moved by nonhuman "animators" (e.g., electronic devices changing the image of the board on the computer screen). The instructions for the moves can also come from computers functioning as the "strategists," while victory or defeat accrues to "principals" who, as owners of the chess-playing computer or shareholders of the company that has produced it, need not even know the rules of the game.

In a later application of frame analysis to verbal communication, Goffman changes the meaning of "figure" and substitutes "author" for "strategist" as one of the four functions.[29] He points out that the "animator" (i.e., the "individual active in the role of speech production") need not be the "author" of the words uttered: he or she may recite a memorized text or read aloud some-

27. It is safe to assume that Goffman would not endorse Amélie Oksenberg Rorty's list of models according to one or another of which we can conceive ourselves as—and thereby actually become—"different entities" with "different properties and proprieties." See "A Literary Postscript: Character, Persons, Selves, Individuals," in *The Identities of Persons*, ed. Amélie Oksenberg Rorty (Berkeley and Los Angeles: University of California Press, 1976), pp. 301–2, where the following menu of options is offered: "heroes, characters, protagonists, actors, agents, persons, souls, selves, figures, individuals." On pp. 318–19 Rorty discusses the additional category of "presences."

28. *Frame Analysis* (note 26 above), esp. pp. 566–76. For brevity's sake, I diverge slightly from Goffman's own illustrative examples of how the four functions operate in professional sports and chess games.

29. Erving Goffman, "Footing" (1979), in his *Forms of Talk* (note 12 to chapter 3), esp. pp. 144–52.

one else's prepared speech. Furthermore, the "animator" or even the "author" need not be the "principal" whose position is established by the words being spoken and who is therefore committed to what the words say; Goffman's examples for the nonidentity of animators, authors, and/or principals include the reading aloud of a deposition by a legal representative and the providing of a simultaneous translation. Finally, Goffman distinguishes between the speaker as "animator" (who may also be "author" and "principal") and the same speaker as "figure"—someone "who belongs to the world spoken about, not to the world in which the speaking occurs." For example, it is the animator who can say very clearly about the figure, "I can't seem to talk clearly today" or even declare, "I am speechless."

Goffman's categories are certainly useful for describing some of the functions discharged by people in mutually recognized frames of social interaction. But they cannot account for the fourfold variety of selves that I cited William James as distinguishing; nor do they encompass our entire "social selves" that James defined as follows: "A man's social self is the recognition which he gets from his mates."[30] Furthermore, the four categories shed little or no light on the past and future history of particular human situations. A functional description of interactive frames is hardly equipped, for example, to deal with the personal motivation of football players who, having initially functioned as "figures" and "animators," may elect to switch frames and serve as their own "strategists." Nor could such a description address issues relating to how the players' decision, once acted upon, will affect future actions undertaken by the coaches as displaced "strategists" and by the fans and club owners as pleased or displeased "principals." That is to say, a snapshot analysis of "frames" cannot help but miss the historical dimension of the complete "pictures" of our lives—those motion pictures, as it were, of human temporality.

30. *The Principles of Psychology* (note 3 to Prologue), 1:293.

## Freedom and Its Discontents

Let me rephrase my main reservations in the vocabulary employed by Beck. The Goffmanian analyst of historically unfolding roles as present functions ends up functioning in the role of *spectator* rather than *critic*. In claiming that culture prescribes "what sort of entity we must believe ourselves to be," he or she reduces the actions performed by personally responsible *agents* to pseudonatural events brought about by causally determined *actors*. More often than not, such an analyst—a self-appointed spectator—fails to ask the troublesome question: Am I myself a determined actor or a responsible agent? Nor is he or she likely to ask: Am I causally determined or free to either ask or not ask questions concerning my own freedom? Are my answers to questions about freedom causally determined or rationally justified?[31]

Clearly, if spectators impute to themselves a measure of freedom and rationality in these matters, it ought to be hard for them to remain confirmed spectators and reduce all other persons to unfree and nonrational actors. Conversely, Beck's critics ought to feel uneasy about deciding case by case who is a determined actor rather than a free rational agent if they attribute their own adoption of such an open-minded position either to causal determination or to free choice. But no proposed solution to the ancient problem of the freedom of the will is likely to escape circular reasoning. Even if I eschew prejudging the issue through prior

31. As the last pair of questions suggests, "causally determined" can be colloquially contrasted either to "free" or to "rationally justified" depending on whether actions (including the speech acts of asking questions) or beliefs (including beliefs verbalized in response to questions) are concerned. In other words, we tend to associate freedom rather than causal determination with rationality. Strictly speaking, however, it is not a belief but the act of holding it that may be a candidate for being either free or causally determined, and it is not the act of holding a belief but the belief that may be a candidate for either being or not being rationally justified. Thus it is logically possible both to be causally determined to hold a rationally justified belief and to be free to hold a belief that is not rationally justified.

commitment to either freedom or determination, I will arrive at indecision through prior commitment to indecision along the following lines: I can't tell whether my or anybody else's will is free because I can't tell whether my holding a particular belief about the matter has or has not been causally determined.

The pertinent quandaries are such that those pondering them may well be excused for being tempted to accept undecidability, declare mystery, or (like John Searle) do both.[32] Searle does the former when he says that he is "unable to reconcile" (p. 86) his commonsense conception of human freedom with his scientific belief in causal determination, and he does the latter when he says: "For reasons that I don't really understand, evolution has given us a form of experience of voluntary action where the experience of freedom, that is to say, the experience of the sense of alternative possibilities, is built into the very structure of conscious, voluntary, intentional human behavior" (p. 98). Like most philosophers addressing the question of free will, Searle contrasts the personal experience of freedom only to natural (as distinct from social) compulsion. Yet something like the human "sense of alternative possibilities"—the ability to imagine and compare different futures—could arise only after the thrust of evolutionary complication had shifted from the mainly natural to the mainly social dimension of being and becoming.

For a very long time in the natural history of life on our planet, the behavior of living organisms was determined by reflex and instinct—rigid stimulus-response patterns that computer engineers might characterize as "hard-wired." Escape your predator, devour your prey, fight your rival, produce sufficient offspring—such were the early, unequivocal imperatives of individual and species survival. At later evolutionary stages, the basic demands for survival would present themselves in increasingly complex combinations and ramifications. To cope with such variety, some

32. John Searle, *Minds, Brains, and Science* (Cambridge: Harvard University Press, 1984), esp. chapter 6, "The Freedom of the Will," pp. 86–99.

species evolved nervous systems capable of selectively mediating between sensory input and motor reaction. The individual organism's capacity for such mediation assumed social significance when, for animals that needed to dwell, travel, or hunt in conspecific groups, the "survival of the fittest" principle began to show its power not only at the individual and the species level but also on the intermediate plane of protosocial formations. Eventually it became efficient for cooperating organisms to develop increasing role differentiation (for example, between leaders and followers or between food gatherers and offspring defenders) so that their group might more easily prevail against other groups of the same as well as other species.[33]

Rudimentary instances of both strategic and gamelike role-playing can be observed among many species of today's animals. The significance of both kinds of role-playing must have been steadily increasing in the lives of our almost human forebears. But a sense of individual freedom is unlikely to have dawned on our predecessors until they had become capable of elementary verbal exchanges about alternative patterns of behavior and about the likely consequences of shifting from one rule or role to another. By the time prehistoric humans routinely found themselves facing role-related alternatives within the range of biologically feasible behaviors, they must have acquired our familiar anxiety of a decreasingly hard-wired creature. How was one to choose, say, between guarding the tribe's fire, joining a war dance in another part of the forest, and going after some plump rabbits in an adjacent field? If grave conse-

33. To be sure, a certain kind of collaborative role differentiation had already occurred when some cells in primitive multicellular organisms began to develop into distinct but interactive organs. From the organ's vantage point one could say that the principles of individuality, society, and nature operate simultaneously whenever the organ performs its particular function within a biological system of role differentiation. But organs don't really have vantage points, of course. Their "individual" contributions to the "social" good of the entire organism merely prefigure, within a mostly "natural" phase of evolutionary history, the subsequent fuller unfolding of the principles of society and individuality.

quences were to be avoided, one needed to have one's role clearly in mind: Was it that of a fire guard? a cultic supplicant? a hunter? To make matters worse, one's role assignment (unlike one's instinctual makeup) could change day by day or even moment by moment, as when an excited fellow tribesman returns to the campsite with news of a beached whale. Should one dare to switch roles, leave the fire unguarded, and join the effort to fight off vultures and other predators eager to consume the whale's eatable parts? If one only knew how the absent chieftain and others would behave, and expect one to behave, in a situation like this!

To put the predicament in more general terms, the choice between or among intersubjectively defined roles often requires the choice maker to engage in extended deliberations. Life, however, goes on even as we weigh the pros and cons of alternative behaviors. Since a lengthy process of deciding between different imagined courses of action renders some options obsolete and others available, the time and energy devoted to personal deliberation becomes an important factor in the natural and social fabric of what is being deliberated about. As a result, we come to feel at least partially empowered—rather than fully determined or inexorably obliged—to behave in certain ways. Natural *must* gives way to social *should* only to make room, eventually, for personal *may* as well.

It is particularly tempting to consider our decisions largely free from natural instinct and even from social pressure when the decisions are made and will be carried out in private situations. For example, my presently deciding not to have a snack after typing this sentence seems to be an obvious instance of the prevalence of personal intention over natural impulse. Yet the superseding of natural desires (e.g., "I want to eat cake") by personal motives (e.g., "I want to be fit and healthy") tends to proceed via internalized social directives (e.g., "It is not popular to be fat"). Furthermore, surviving individuals must have been making, and extant societies must have been obliging their members to make, relatively few choices against the grain of natural prescriptions, or else the individuals and societies in question would not have survived.

As societies become increasingly complicated, individuals have to make more and more choices among the different role-connected *oughts* according to which different people, as well as the "generalized other," expect them to act. Indeed, complex modern and postmodern societies offer many of their members a disquietingly wide range of choices among numerous role-connected but seldom fully prescribed types of behavior. As a result, such societies impose on private reflection the unfinishable task of continually evaluating the roles that the individual in question has been or might have been playing.[34] But a person's evaluations of his or her roles—and of the natural, social, and personal motives for playing them—exert a decisive impact on just "who" that person is and wants to become.[35] More than anything else, our vividly experienced capacity for consequential self-evaluation makes virtually all of us feel free and, therefore, responsible. At the same time, many of us occasionally wonder whether we are really free or have the perhaps unwarranted experience of being free only because neurophysiological laws constrain us or intersubjectively shared personal delusions incline us to have it.

34. According to Jürgen Habermas, "Moral Development and Ego Identity," in his *Communication and the Evolution of Society*, trans. Thomas McCarthy (Boston: Beacon, 1979), p. 78 et passim, all commitment to moral principles should remain open to further reflection about "needs that still await suitable interpretation."

35. See Charles Taylor, "Responsibility for Self," in *The Identities of Persons*, ed. Amélie Oksenberg Rorty (Berkeley and Los Angeles: University of California Press, 1976), pp. 281–99, reprinted in *Free Will*, ed. Gary Watson (London: Oxford University Press, 1982), pp. 122–23: "Our strong evaluations . . . are attempts to formulate what is initially inchoate, or confused, or badly formulated. But this kind of formulation or reformulation doesn't leave its objects unchanged. To give a certain articulation is to shape our sense of what we desire or what we hold important in a certain way." See also Harry G. Frankfurt, "Freedom of the Will and the Concept of a Person," *Journal of Philosophy* 68 (1971): 5–20, likewise reprinted in *Free Will*, pp. 82–83: "One essential difference between persons and other creatures is to be found in the structure of a person's will. Human beings . . . are capable of wanting to be different, in their preferences and purposes, from what they are."

In any case, the self-making power of reflective evaluation, about which more will be said in the next chapter, goes a long way toward explaining why our strong sense of freedom remains largely unaffected even by the most forceful intellectual arguments against it on behalf of divine predestination, natural causation, or the social construction of reality. But the case against freedom has shown similar tenacity. Antilibertarians of all stripes manage to disregard their own subjective experience of freedom in order to maintain a religious or secular faith in determinism. On the religious side, such faith ranges from devoutly strict fatalism concerning every microcosmic detail to a more relaxed belief in broadly based providential governance. Secular determinism in turn spans the parallel distance from ironclad belief in total causation to a more relaxed espousal of theories concerning the statistical probability of certain natural or social occurrences. Clearly enough, however, all varieties of determinism restrict human freedom more than human experience appears to warrant. I believe, therefore, that John Searle's unanswered question of why "evolution has given us" an experience of freedom should be seen as complementary to the much more neglected question: *Why has evolution also given us the antilibertarian urge to defy that experience?*

It is true that the survival of the human species up until now indicates that the kinds of things individual humans need to do in order to survive can be done best—or perhaps can only be done—with the agent's subjective sense of personal freedom. But the frequent clashes, both in mental and in public deliberations, between libertarianism and determinism have not proved detrimental to human survival either. I rather suspect that a composite of the two kinds of worldview best promotes the well-being of both individuals and societies. After all, it is only an intertwining of libertarian and deterministic attitudes that entitles us to the remarkable (and apparently life-promoting) flexibility with which we tend to assign credit and blame for the consequences of actions to responsible human agents on the one hand and to the natural, supernatural, or institutional "puppeteers" of marionette-like human actors on the other.[36]

I am not urging that the feeling of personal freedom and a concomitant tendency to renounce that feeling had to be a pair of required traits, jointly selected for in surviving human populations. The copresence of the two attitudes may well have been a vicarious evolutionary by-product of the increase in verbal skills that gave some early human communities a competitive edge of superior cooperation and superior intelligence over others. People routinely participating in articulate public deliberations about cooperative action could both develop a strong sense of freedom and become prone to ponder how the frequent frustration of human plans and hopes limits the efficacy of our experienced freedom. They could thus evolve a mixed attitude to individual self-determination and transmit that mixed attitude culturally through the contrastive wisdom of myths and adages like the familiar pair "Where there's a will, there's a way" and "Man proposes, God disposes."

## Liberation through Diversity

Prehistoric speculation aside, it seems clear that our subjective sense of personal freedom and responsibility is to this day deeply rooted in our (biologically imposed) need to play social roles and in our (biologically bequeathed) capacity to conduct intersubjective conversations about them. In other words, we are objectively

---

36. I derive the image of several puppeteers pulling the strings of powerless human beings from Shaw's preface to *Saint Joan*. In the section "A Void in the Elizabethan Drama," the playwright claims that his audiences "will have before them not only the visible and human puppets, but the Church, the Inquisition, the Feudal System, with divine inspiration always beating against their too inelastic limits: all more terrible in their dramatic force than any of the little mortal figures clanking about in plate armor or moving silently in the frocks and hoods of the order of St. Dominic." See Bernard Shaw, *Collected Plays with Their Prefaces*, vol. 6 (London: Bodley Head, 1973), p. 71.

equipped and intersubjectively socialized to ponder and debate subjective alternatives—including alternative answers to the question whether nature forces, society prompts, or personal identity inspires each of us to give a particular answer to this very question. Hence the paradox: nature and, to some extent, society appear to compel each human self to exist in relative independence from such compulsion.

Mindful of the constant interplay of doing, making, and meaning in all culture, existence, and experience, we should, of course, avoid assuming that we are "made"—both created and compelled—to do what we only appear to mean to. Such an assumption would amount to supposing that at the "most fundamental level" of objective existence natural or supernatural determination reigns supreme and that our sense of freedom at the social and individual levels of intersubjective culture and subjective experience stems from delusion. I see no reason for thus reducing both the domain of interpersonal activity and the domain of personal identity to the domain of impersonal facticity. After all, those subscribing to the view that our sense of freedom is illusory are likely to claim that their adoption of such a view is rationally justified rather than a mere effect of biological cause or social purpose. Likewise, most of my readers are probably convinced that they are free to assess the validity of what I am saying here rather than causally or teleologically compelled to accept or reject my argument without good reason. Yet the very case for determination or coercion becomes destabilized each time it is being personally considered as valid or invalid for good reason, because the personal freedom to accept or reject an argument for good reason is no small matter. People will act differently if they think differently. Even as organisms they are what they are because, as players of social roles and bearers of personal self-consciousness, they act and think in certain ways rather than in others. Intersubjective activity and subjective identity may thus be historically emergent aspects of objective facticity, but having emerged, both find themselves in constant dialectic interplay with each other and the latter. That is to say, the social, the natural or supernatural, and the personal are complementary dimensions of being human, not hierarchical levels of cause-driven or goal-directed compulsion by causal or teleological forces foreign to human culture, existence, and experience.

Needless to say, the human species as we know it will not survive forever. Perhaps a breed of extraterrestrial others will ascribe our extinction or radical transformation to some natural catastrophe (for example, to the collision of a large comet with the Earth). But I like to imagine them wondering whether what undid us was our belief in determination, our "unrenounceable" experience of freedom, or else the "cognitive dissonance" between our deterministic and libertarian attitudes.[37] Meanwhile human experience, culture, and existence remain defined by the simultaneous relevance to them of what each of us may, ought to, and must do. We would cease to be humans if we no longer felt that each of us has a measure of personal freedom not to follow the dictates of nature and society even if noncompliance may turn out to be lethal.

All the same, most of us are often tempted to narrow our focus and recognize only one or two of the three principal components of the human condition: natural or supernatural determination, social interdependence, and personal freedom. There are rewards for doing so. By denying determination, we turn away from the objective reality of finitude and death. By denying interdependence, we avoid seeing the intersubjective reality of competition and conflict. By denying freedom, we refuse to accept the subjective reality of isolation and responsibility. As I suggested in the

37. In *Freedom and Belief* (Oxford: Clarendon, 1986), Galen Strawson points out that our "unrenounceable commitment" to a subjective sense of freedom persists in the teeth of overwhelming objective evidence against the "possibility of self-determination" (see esp. pp. 74–83). He also surveys a great deal of current and earlier work, some of which is quite technical, on the relevant philosophical issues. I borrow the phrase "cognitive dissonance" from the title of Leon Festinger, *A Theory of Cognitive Dissonance* (Evanston, Ill.: Row, Peterson, 1957).

Prologue, it is relatively easy to subscribe to just one totalizing tenet like "It's all in the genes," "Individuals are mere products of their society," or "Every person is a fully autonomous moral agent." It is much harder to confront simultaneously the darker side of each of the three giant claims. Yet the unflinching recognition of all such human predicaments as finitude, death, competition, conflict, isolation, and responsibility seems to be required if we are to thrive in our ever more precarious being of, with, and toward a radically plural world.[38]

We like to think that our sense of living in a plural world is "postmodern." But some Greek Sophists, German romanticists, and American pragmatists, as well as many skeptics of all climes and ages, seem to have felt similarly engulfed by "a *plural*istic *uni*verse."[39] In worlds inviting such oxymoronic characterization, the principles of nature, self, and society (the One as Many, the One as One, and the Many as One) point beyond themselves to the fourth principle invoked at the beginning of this chapter: radical diversity, or the principle of the Many as Many. Far from claiming to reconcile or dialectically sublate its rivals, the fourth principle leaves each to predominate in its respective domain as first among equals. In the domain of humanity-making nature, we thus find ourselves determined by physical forces and biological instincts; in the domain of human-made culture, we find ourselves directed by social roles and institutional rules; in the domain of evolving (and therefore always self-transcending) self-hood, we find ourselves propelled by personal motives and transpersonal aspirations. In other words, we gain access to our intertwined existence, culture, and experience through what constitutes them in the first place—our natural being of, social being

38. The increasing need for sufficient degrees of existential correspondence, cultural consensus, and experiential coherence—those never fully attained goals of our cognitive, conative, and emotive orientations—will be discussed in the last section of the next chapter.

39. The quoted phrase, to which I have added the italics, served as the title of a 1909 lecture series by William James.

with, and personal being toward the world. By contrast, the "domain" of diversity is ubiquitous but elusive. It is, indeed, a nondomain to which our access must always remain indirect, since the fourth principle manifests itself *ironically*—through the partial invalidity of all four and any other principles.[40]

Nonetheless, the recognition that a fourth principle limits the share of natural facticity, social activity, and personal identity in the governance of our lives can greatly help to modify our understanding of determination, interdependence, and freedom. No one seems to doubt that his or her personal freedom is exercised under certain natural and social constraints. Yet nature and society need not be seen as enemies of freedom, because freedom, in the sense of situated autonomy, is by no means confined to the personal domain. The free development of a society can, for instance, be obstructed by such natural and personal impediments as frequent droughts causing poor harvests or a powerful ruler's stubborn refusal to compromise. Nature's free development is in turn blocked occasionally by social forces or individual atrocities. For example, the profit-hungry tuna industry may eliminate dol-

---

40. I speak of irony in the sense in which Kenneth Burke and Hayden White contrast it as the trope of dialectic reversal to three other "master tropes": metaphor, metonymy, and synecdoche. Their view of irony as ultimately self-critical—rather than just critical of other attempts at what Burke calls "the discovery and description of 'the truth' " (p. 503)—has helped me to appreciate the paradoxical triumph of diversity over nature, society, and individuality. The Pyrrhic victory of that "fourth principle" lies in its proving to be the radically other—the exception to any principle whatever. See Kenneth Burke, *A Grammar of Motives* (1945; Berkeley and Los Angeles: University of California Press, 1969), app. D, "Four Master Tropes," pp. 503–17, and Hayden White, *Metahistory: The Historical Imagination in Nineteenth-Century Europe* (Baltimore: Johns Hopkins University Press, 1973), esp. pp. 31–38. An early contraposition of irony to metaphor, metonymy, and synecdoche can be found in Giambattista Vico, *The New Science* (1744), trans. Thomas Godard Bergin and Max Harold Fisch, 3d ed. (Ithaca: Cornell University Press, 1968), pp. 127–31. For further comment on Burke's ideas about irony, see my "Literary Interpretation and the Rhetoric of Human Sciences," in *The Rhetoric of the Human Sciences: Language and Argument in Scholarship and Public Affairs*, ed. John S. Nelson, Alan Megill, and Donald N. McCloskey (Madison: University of Wisconsin Press, 1987), pp. 271–72 and p. 275 n. 17.

phins before they could become a more intelligent species, and a deranged baby-sitter may drown a supremely gifted infant who could otherwise have prevented some disease from wiping out millions of human organisms. Less exotic examples might no doubt be found to illustrate my point: rather than seeing nature, society, and individuality as unequally powerful agents of absolute compulsion, we should learn to appreciate the relative autonomy and mutual impact of all three dimensions of our existence, culture, and experience. After all, being situated by nature and society means external imposition of force only so long as I remain alienated from the transactions whereby my existence and culture manifest their reciprocally constrained power of self-determination in and through my personal experience.

To diminish the bite of such alienation, we may strive to envision and deserve a kind of freedom that is no longer narrowly personal. Such freedom—an ironic rather than a heroic sort—would entail playing out the relative autonomies of our natural, social, and personal modes of being and becoming against each other. The personal chances of success for this kind of profound liberation depend on the extent to which a particular *I*'s sense of *we* manages to regather all *thou*s and *it*s of a lifeworld as fragments of primary *I-Thou* and *I-It* relations—diverse aspects of mutual compulsion through reciprocally situated freedoms. Ultimately, however, every person capable of saying "we" needs to learn to accept—not necessarily to like—what all of us including galaxies and bacteria separately are if "we" are to become *us* in the fullest ecumenical sense of intertwined diversity ascribed to those shifting pronouns in the previous chapter.

# Chapter Five

# Four More Triads and Beyond

At various points in this book's rethinking of culture, existence, and experience, I have linked up those elongated shadows of doing, making, and meaning with the following triads: (1) speaking, writing, and thinking as exemplary vehicles of intersubjective communication, objectifying expression, and subjectifying representation; (2) second-, third-, and first-person views of life as complementary horizons of the role-players, organisms, and selves that human beings simultaneously are; and (3) social activity, natural facticity, and personal identity as intertwined dimensions of our being with, of, and toward the world.

In the present chapter, I apply the conceptual framework developed so far to three historically significant triads: (1) moving, delighting, and teaching—the principal aims of discourse emerging from the rhetorical tradition of Greco-Roman antiquity and the European Renaissance; (2) willing, feeling, and knowing—the human "faculties" or "capacities" to which Kant's three *Critiques* hitched the philosophical disciplines of ethics, aesthetics, and epistemology; and (3) justice, beauty, and truth—a trinity of "supreme values" often assumed to stem from ancient Greek thought but in obvious need of both historical and theoretical reconsideration.

The first three sections of the chapter explore the contemporary relevance of the three traditional triads. Each of these sections includes a chart highlighting the relationships—by no means simple parallels—between some historically significant concerns and some more obviously current ones. Such charts necessarily simplify and, abstracted from the accompanying narrative, can easily serve as sitting pigeons for critical target practice. Furthermore, each of the three charts might appear to my more "ancient" readers as newfangled and to my more "modern" or "postmodern" readers as old-fashioned. I take those risks in the hope that the graphic representation helps to clarify the advantages of thinking about culture, existence, and experience within more than one conceptual framework. In the fourth, final section I introduce yet another triad: cultural consensus, experiential coherence, and environmental (that is to say, existential) congruence or correspondence. Consensus, coherence, and correspondence have sometimes been invoked as rival criteria of truth. From the present book, they should emerge rather as mutually supportive goals in our lifelong pursuit of interactive doing, self-expressive making, and world-oriented meaning.

## To Move, Delight, and Teach

The three traditional aims of rhetoric are easily aligned with action, production, and signification even beyond the scope of strictly verbal practice. Consider the relationship of a speech, a song, a building, or a motion picture to its audience. In a broad sense, each "moves" its respective recipients as a "thing done" to them; each "delights" its recipients as a "thing made" for them; each "teaches" its recipients as a "thing meant" (that is, mentally processed) by them. But the respective linkages established in earlier chapters between doing and society, between making and nature, and between meaning and selfhood are destabilized in the present context. As the accompanying chart should help us realize, natural facticity tends to predominate in some moving (arousal of passions) but also in some delighting (appeal to the senses); social activity tends to predominate in some moving (political agitation) but also in some teaching (guidance for interactive conduct); and individual identity tends to predominate in some teaching (personally attested evidence) but also in some delighting (swaying a particular self into person-to-person or person-to-cosmos acquiescence).

In mapping the relationships just outlined, figure 1 suggests that the influential threesome of rhetorical aims named by Quintilian as *movere, delectare,* and *docere* (3.5.2) need not eliminate the productive tension between Cicero's two divergent listings of the effective speaker's threefold objectives: *movere, conciliare,* and *docere* or stir, win over, and instruct in *De oratore,* (2.18.121); *flectere, delectare,* and *probare* or steer, please, and prove in *Orator* (p. 69).[1] Later theorists of rhetoric preserved the tension more conspicuously in the first-named area than in the other two. Most of their references to "teaching" fuse moral instruction (*docere*) with persuasive demonstration (*probare*), and their typical notion of "delighting" combines winning over, swaying, or even appeasing (*conciliare*) with titillation of some kind (*delectare*). By contrast, the "moving" function of discourse tends to get divided into the di-

1. The crucial sentence in the bilingual edition of *The "Institutio Oratoria" of Quintilian,* trans. H. E. Butler, 4 vols (Cambridge: Harvard University Press, 1920), 1:396, reads: "Tria sunt item, quae praestare debeat orator, ut doceat, moveat, delectet." Even Cicero was not consistent, however, in splitting each of the three major rhetorical aims into two. The different triads cited above from *De oratore* and *Orator* are not exclusively employed in either work; *probare* rather than *docere* occurs at 2.27.115 of *De oratore,* for example. Furthermore, Quintilian's single triad is anticipated in the following sentence, attributed to Cicero without precise source reference in George Campbell, *The Philosophy of Rhetoric* (1776; Carbondale: Southern Illinois University Press, 1962, p.1 n. 1): "Optimus est orator qui dicendo animos audientium et docet, et delectat, et permovet."

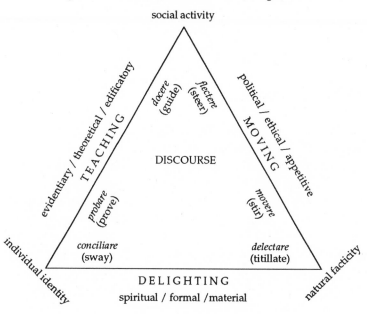

Figure 1. Three aims of discourse: move, delight, teach

dactic and the passionate—the high-minded edificatory goal of *flectere* in the sense of "bend" or "steer" and the rather suspect capacity of *movere* as "stir" or "arouse."

Philip Sidney's *Apology for Poetry* (1583) may serve as an example of the privileging of the first kind of impact ( *flectere*) over the second kind (*movere*). Writing in a period of increasingly passionate attacks by Puritan preachers on the passions, Sidney praises only the edificatory kind of moving (i.e., a careful steering) as "well nigh the cause and the effect of teaching."[2] There is no defense in the *Apology* of the irresistible "transport" that Longinus enthusiastically ascribed, with explicit depreciation of mere "persuasion" or "gratification," to the sublime orator's effect on an

2. Sir Philip Sidney, *An Apology for Poetry*, ed. Forrest G. Robinson (Indianapolis: Bobbs-Merrill, 1970), p. 37.

audience.[3] In today's parlance, Sidney attributes poetry's value to its unrivaled potential not so much to *move* as to *motivate* us "with desire to know" and also "to do that which we know" (p. 38). He asks: "For who will be taught if he be not moved with desire to be taught, and what so much good doth that teaching bring forth (I speak still of moral doctrine) as that it moveth one to do that which it doth teach?" (p. 37).

Some later writers extend the domain of moving to include ethical or political motivation on the one hand and the arousal of passions or appetites on the other.[4] Others in turn distinguish material, spiritual, and formal delights as respective triggers of sensory pleasure, the serene bliss of moral or religious beatitude, and the aesthetic appreciation of "pure" beauty.[5] Comparably broad distinctions in the domain of teaching might contrast furnishing particular evidence and outlining a general argument or theory to the edificatory guiding of conduct ranging from cookbooks to the Ten Commandments. Most ancient as well as modern surveys of the aims of verbal communication have, however, remained content with just the basic tripartite system of moving, teaching, and delighting. One reason for this may well be that such a threefold classification of aims nicely parallels Aristotle's basic divi-

3. See section 1 of *Longinus on the Sublime*, ed. and trans. W. Rhys Roberts (Cambridge: Cambridge University Press, 1899), esp. p. 43.

4. For example, George Campbell's *The Philosophy of Rhetoric* (see note 1 above) assigns instrumental value to the passions: "The passions are the natural spurs to volition or action, and so need only to be right directed" (p. 2). At a time of heightened "sentiment" and "sensibility"—with reference to Germany, the 1770s and 1780s are often called the period of storm and stress—Campbell names four rather than only three "ends of speaking" to which all others are "reducible," namely, "to enlighten the understanding, to please the imagination, to move the passions, or to influence the will" (p. 1). I would argue that the separate listing of the last two goals spells out Cicero's distinction between *movere* and *flectere*.

5. Kant's *Critique of Judgment* (1790) comes readily to mind as the fountainhead of post-Enlightenment efforts to exclude "mere" pleasantness (*das Angenehme*), as well as both instrumental and "sheer" goodness (*das schlechterdings . . . Gute*), from the purview of aesthetics properly concerned with the "pure" beauty of forms. See esp. part 1, sections 3 and 4 in Immanuel Kant, *Critique of Judgment*, trans. Werner S. Pluhar (Indianapolis: Hackett, 1987), pp. 47–53.

sion of rhetorical practice (*Rhetoric* 1.3) into three kinds: the deliberative (persuasion to a course of action), the forensic (persuasion by evidentiary proof), and the epideictic (persuasion through lavish praise or blame).[6]

To be sure, relatively few instances of speaking actually occur in such strictly "Aristotelian" situations as parliamentary assemblies, law courts, or memorial services. Furthermore, the chiefly steering, proving, and pleasing aims of deliberative, forensic, and epideictic discourses are eminently combinable. For example, the trial lawyer's evidentiary proof is meant to steer the jury or the judge toward a consequential decision, and the poet's ode can simultaneously delight and inculcate moral values. Yet the primary function of most oral and written discourses seems to have remained to elicit action, impart knowledge, or provide pleasure by committing, informing, or entertaining an audience. Hence the continued relevance of the double-headed triad of classical rhetoric to most communicative occasions including everyday private conversations. We need to steer (*flectere*) as well as stir (*movere*) if we are to commit a decision-making audience of one or more persons to consequential intentions. We need to articulate the implications (*docere*) of plausibly presented evidence (*probare*) if we are to convince a judging audience to share our interpretation of a state of affairs. And we need to appeal both to senses (*delectare*) and to sensibilities (*conciliare*) if we are to rivet the attention of an as yet unfocused audience to our verbal display.

It is indeed quite usual for one of the three chief aims of classical orators to predominate in a particular type of cultural practice. For example, religious and political leaders are mainly expected to inspire commitment, while scientists and news re-

6. George A. Kennedy, *Classical Rhetoric and Its Christian and Secular Tradition from Ancient to Modern Times* (Chapel Hill: University of North Carolina Press, 1980), p. 100, also links the Ciceronian triad of proving, winning over, and passionate appeal (*De oratore* 2.27.115) to Aristotle's three means of "proof"— the *logos* of coherent argument, the speaker's impressive *ethos*, and the arousal of the listener's *pathos*.

porters are mainly expected to provide information. Most explicit "defenses" of poetry and other arts tend to subordinate the delighting function to an obligation to teach[7] or even derive the experienced pleasure from the process of learning.[8] Since, however, practitioners of the arts have long been expected to offer entertainment, delight did find some unembarrassed partisans of its own. John Dryden, perhaps following Ludovico Castelvetro's commentary (1576) on Aristotle's *Poetics*, explicitly stated: "Delight is the chief, if not the only end of Poesie; instruction can be admitted but in the second place, for Poesie only instructs as it delights."[9] And William Wordsworth even insisted that "the poet writes under one restriction only, namely, the necessity of giving immediate pleasure to a human being."[10]

Needless to say, many instances of purported teaching, delighting, and moving sooner or later strike us as erroneous, trivial, or misdirected. Why, then, the urge to engage in such risky activities as listening, reading, theatergoing, television watching, and the like? We have an obvious social need to remain in touch with each other, but we also seek information, entertainment, and

7. Recall Samuel Johnson's famous dictum from the preface to his edition of Shakespeare's works: "The end of writing is to instruct; the end of poetry is to instruct by pleasing." *The Yale Edition of the Works of Samuel Johnson*, vol. 7, ed. Arthur Sherbo (New Haven: Yale University Press, 1968), p. 67.

8. As does Aristotle in chapter 4 of his *Poetics* (1448b).

9. Quoted from Dryden's 1668 "defense" of his *Essay of Dramatic Poesy* in the preface to *The Indian Emperour*; see *The Works of John Dryden*, vol. 9, ed. John Loftis (Berkeley and Los Angeles: University of California Press, 1966), pp. 5–6. For Castelvetro, an articulate Renaissance defender of pleasure against teaching as a "false goal" of poetry, see Marvin Carlson, *Theories of the Theatre* (Ithaca: Cornell University Press, 1984), p. 48.

10. See the 1850 edition of Wordsworth's much revised "Preface" to the 2d edition (1800) of his and Coleridge's *Lyrical Ballads*, quoted from *The Prose Works of William Wordsworth*, ed. W. J. B. Owen and Jane Worthington Smyser, vol. 1 (Oxford: Clarendon, 1974), p. 139. Wordsworth goes on to claim that the orientation toward delighting should be regarded not "as a degradation of the poet's art" but rather as "an acknowledgment of the beauty of the universe, . . . a homage paid to the native and naked dignity of man, to the grand elementary principle of pleasure, by which he knows, and feels, and lives, and moves" (p. 140).

commitment for the personal reason of wanting to escape the experience of ignorance, boredom, and indifference. Those three nearly vacant states of mind—the zero degrees, respectively, of knowledge, feeling, and will—bring us as close as living persons can possibly come to a harrowing sense of nonexistence. The thrill of approaching without reaching one of the three kinds of mental void is, of course, the fire that some self-congratulatory practitioners of skepticism, apathy, and indecision enjoy playing with. In contrast to ignorance, boredom, and indifference, even inaccurate information, trivial entertainment, and ill-advised commitment can heighten our sense of being alive: they invigorate us by making us believe, feel, or desire. After considering various kinds of belief, feeling, and desire in the next section of this chapter, I will briefly return to teaching, delighting, and moving in the context of the third section's threefold theme of truth, beauty, and justice.

## Willing, Feeling, Knowing

Introspection suggests that knowing, feeling, and willing are roughly distinguishable from each other despite the considerable variety of the mental processes encompassed by each term or by their Latinate equivalents—cognition, emotion, and conation. I reluctantly adopt the term "conation" from the technical language of psychology because, unlike the more familiar word "volition," it encompasses both impulsive desire and deliberate will. For most purposes of this chapter it is appropriate to eschew sharp initial distinctions not only between desire and will but also between belief and knowledge and between primary feeling and transferential empathy. After all, the following assumptions strike me as eminently justified: (1) Participatory intentions often prompt us to altruistic acts that, *pace* Kant, simultaneously involve both will to duty and desire stemming from inclination. (2) In the absence of certain knowledge, the cognitive value of unfalsified beliefs reflecting widely shared opinions should, *pace* Plato, not be disparaged. (3) Natural empathy and culturally trained imagination permit each of us to feel not only *for* but also *as* another person; the very experience of a "me" evolves, as Mead has argued, out of empathically adopting the attitude of others toward oneself.[11]

If I were to assign temporal priority to a particular type of awareness, I would surmise in the Epicurean tradition that feelings of pleasure and pain (or of comfort and discomfort) lie at the root of all sentient life. Even organisms on precognitive and preconative rungs of the evolutionary ladder presumably register changes in their well-being through rudimentary analogues of the human feelings of satisfaction and dissatisfaction. Likewise, human infants presumably feel the difference between comfort and discomfort (including pain) long before their mental life becomes articulated into a single subject and sundry objects of potential knowledge or desire. In a sense, therefore, emotive awareness initiates the dialectical process through which the self and its world "make" each other so that the former may begin to "mean" and "do"—both cognize and act upon the latter.

On further reflection, however, it seems more accurate to consider all three types of mentation as incipiently present in any kind of primitive awareness that can be imputed to an organism. After all, who would seriously propose to distinguish different kinds of "mental orientation" when a particular lizard appears to seek, recognize, and enjoy sunshine? Only higher mammals and birds, whose species-specific interaction with their natural and social surroundings has reached a certain level of complexity, seem capable of shifting the focus of their awareness between protocognitive "knowledge" of just what has gratified or hurt

11. Kant's sharp contrast between duty and inclination pervades his *Critique of Practical Reason;* for Plato's sharp contrast between knowledge and opinion, see *Phaedrus* 247, 248, and *Republic* 5:476–78, 6:508D, 510A, 7:534; for Mead on the emergence of the self, see above, chapter 4, second section.

them and protoconative "desire" for objects and situations that might increase or decrease their protoemotive "feelings" of pleasure and pain. I use quotation marks in the previous sentence to indicate that I attribute knowing, desiring, and feeling to animal species through anthropomorphic projection. But I also believe that unconditionally rejecting all such projections would entail the unjustified assumption of radical discontinuity between humans and the rest of nature.

To whatever extent nonhuman organisms feel, know, and will, this much seems certain: Human survival has long depended on our ability to focus selectively on what we feel (sensation and emotion), what appears to be eliciting that feeling (cognition), and what must be done to prolong or change it (conation). On a post-Darwinian view, the current degree of marked differentiation between human emotion, cognition, and conation can indeed be attributed to evolutionary selection. Some protohuman organisms must have been more capable than others of promptly responding to the changing circumstances of their lives by channeling appropriate amounts of biological energy in the respectively required directions of knowing, willing, *or* feeling. These versatile creatures would then survive and reproduce with greater statistical frequency than their conspecific rivals. Hence the eventual trifurcation into the mental "faculties" or "capacities" for which Kant coined the German names *Erkenntnisvermögen* (the ability to cognize), *Begehrungsvermögen* (the ability to desire and will), and *Gefühl der Lust und Unlust* (feeling of pleasure and displeasure).[12]

12. See section 3 of the second introduction to Immanuel Kant, *Kritik der Urteilskraft* (1790), 4th ed., ed. Karl Vorländer (Leipzig: Meiner, 1913), p. 13; English version: *Critique of Judgment*, trans. Werner S. Pluhar (Indianapolis: Hackett, 1987), p. 16: "For all of the soul's powers or capacities can be reduced to three that cannot be derived further from a common basis: the *cognitive power*, the *feeling of pleasure and displeasure*, and the *power of desire*." At the individual level, the species-specific disjunction of the three orientations may be linked to such neurological changes in each evolving human brain as are postulated by Gerald Edelman, *Neural Darwinism: The Theory of Neuronal Group Selection* (New York: Basic Books, 1987).

To be sure, the cognitive processing of information tends to direct awareness away from the self and the emotive experiencing of satisfaction or dissatisfaction directs awareness toward it. Yet it would be wrong to think of cognition as "objective" and of emotion as "subjective" in a simplistic sense of those often misused words. After all, cognition does not afford direct access to the "objective" reality of some self-sufficient realm of quasi-Platonic Being, nor are human emotions "subjective" in the sense of being haphazard occurrences in a monadic individual. Rather, knowing subjectifies—integrates within a particular mind—aspects of the world's multiplicity, and feeling objectifies—rivets to a single target of attention—the organism's initially inchoate response to its environment. Willing in turn shapes our ways of interacting with other people and with non-human entities that—from worshiped deities to hard-to-open parcels—are sometimes perceived as responsive or resistant conative agents. On such a view our cognitive, emotive, and conative orientations are continually trying to make the objective, subjective, and intersubjective dimensions of world and self better "match" each other.[13] That is to say, nature, identity, and society—three rather than the two hands of the Escher drawing invoked at the end of my Prologue—keep sketching one another as they both give rise to and emerge from our acts of knowing, feeling, and willing.

13. As early as in 1856 John Ruskin complained: "German dullness, and English affectation, have of late much multiplied among us the use of two of the most objectionable words that were ever coined by the troublesomeness of metaphysicians—namely, 'objective' and 'subjective.' " In the ensuing paragraphs Ruskin notes that gunpowder has "a power of exploding" even if it does not explode because you have "put no match to it." With a nice play on the word "match," he concludes: "If you find that you cannot explode the gunpowder, you will not declare that all gunpowder is subjective . . . but you will simply suspect and declare yourself to be an ill-made match." Cf. Ruskin's "Of the Pathetic Fallacy," quoted from John Ruskin, *Modern Painters*, vol. 3 in *The Works of John Ruskin*, ed. E. T. Cook and Alexander Wedderburn (London: Allen, 1904), 5:201–3. For more about my view of the cultural practices of subjectifying representation, objectifying expression, and intersubjective communication, see chapter 1 above, third and fourth sections.

I realize, of course, that many contemporary psychologists and philosophers doubt whether Kant's triad of the knowing, feeling, and willing "faculties" exhausts all, or at least properly distinguishes most, phenomena of human mentation. Even Jerome Bruner, who appears friendly toward the underlying tripartition, cautions readers of his book *Actual Minds, Possible Worlds:* "The components of the behavior I am speaking of are not emotions, cognitions, and actions, each in isolation, but aspects of a larger whole that achieves its integration only within a cultural system. . . . All three terms represent abstractions. . . . The price we pay for such abstractions in the end is to lose sight of their structural interdependence."[14] Mindful of Bruner's warning about the "high theoretical cost" of such abstractions, I have devised the accompanying chart precisely to stress the "structural interdependence" of emotion, cognition, and conation—not as distinct mental faculties but as alternate predominant types of embodied awareness. Rather than suggest a rigid scheme of distinct mental subfaculties, figure 2 is intended to show how different types of awareness blend into each other: certain varieties of both feeling and desire are primarily linked to our natural being *of* the world; certain varieties of both feeling and knowledge are primarily linked to our personal being *toward* the world, and certain varieties of both knowledge and desire are primarily linked to our social being *with* the world.

The chart no doubt simplifies the complex mental phenomena involved, particularly if the terms correlated in it are not understood in the context established for them in the previous and ensuing paragraphs. For example, "desire" covers the entire continuum from impulsive to participatory conation,[15] and "know-

14. Jerome Bruner, *Actual Minds, Possible Worlds* (Cambridge: Harvard University Press, 1986), pp. 117–18.
15. I share Harry G. Frankfurt's concern for the "established nuances" of words like "want" and "desire"—one might add "wish," "will," and a few others. But I also follow him in using such words almost "interchangeably" in part because, to quote Frankfurt, "the verb 'to want,' which suits my purposes better so far as its meaning is concerned, does not lend itself so readily to the formation of nouns as does the verb 'to desire.' " See Frankfurt (note 35 to chapter 4), p. 83 n. 2.

*Figure 2.* Three types of awareness: conation, emotion, cognition

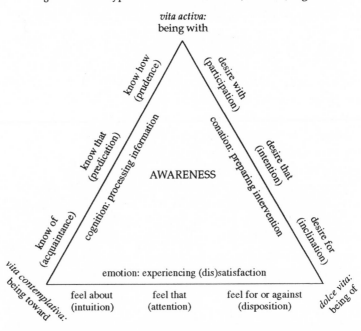

*vita activa:*
being with

know how
(prudence)

desire with
(participation)

know that
(predication)

cognition: processing information

AWARENESS

conation: preparing intervention

desire that
(intention)

desire for
(inclination)

know of
(acquaintance)

*vita contemplativa:*
being toward

emotion: experiencing (dis)satisfaction

feel about
(intuition)

feel that
(attention)

feel for or against
(disposition)

*dolce vita:*
being of

ing" stands for any cognitive orientation toward an individually experienced and intersubjectively validated reality, not for some angelic vision of truth independent of human feelings and desires. Furthermore, I do not wish to invoke all connotations of *vita contemplativa* and *vita activa* in ancient and medieval philosophy when I borrow those Latin terms to designate the directions in which the respective combinations of knowing and feeling and of knowing and desire orient us. By contrast, the contact point of feeling and desire is named with specific reference to Federico Fellini's 1960 movie *La dolce vita* about a "sweet" or bittersweet way of aimlessly drifting life—too shallow and narrow to become profoundly "contemplative" or comprehensively "active."

At the center of the baseline of the triangle, the word "attention" refers to the human organism's ability to transform a set of corporeal microevents into a single experienced feeling of general comfort or discomfort. When attention begins to focus on something external, the attentive *feeling that* emotive satisfaction or dissatisfaction is occurring turns into an intuitive *feeling about*, or else into a dispositional *feeling for* or *against*, whatever appears to trigger the felt (dis)satisfaction. Since intuition and disposition clearly are forms of incipient knowledge and desire, no mental barrier separates the emotive orientation of awareness from its cognitive or conative counterparts, to the first of which we now turn.

Moving upward on the left side of the chart from chiefly contemplative acquaintance (the *knowing of* an object or an objectified person) toward the practical wisdom of *knowing how* to engage in some activity, we pass through opinion or belief—the *knowing that* such and such is (stipulated to be) the case.[16] In other words, the road from contemplation to action—from the private towardness of perceptual acquaintance to the public witness of skillful prudence—leads through knowledge of the kind that can be shared in predicative sentences (e.g., "Snow is white"). I consider predicative or propositional knowledge the "central" or prototypical phase of cognitively processing information because, as a rule, it is less affected by emotion than is acquaintance and less connected to conation than is prudence. In positive terms one might

16. Concerning the difference between acquaintance and belief (or between what I respectively call "knowing of" and "knowing that"), see Bertrand Russell, *The Problems of Philosophy* (1912; paperback ed. New York: Oxford University Press, 1959), esp. pp. 119–21. By "knowing how" I refer to the complete range of such learned skills as repairing bicycles, doing long division, observing a dress code, or engaging in conversation—anything that enables us, in a sense broader than Wittgenstein's, "to go on" with our lives. Cf. section 154 et passim in Ludwig Wittgenstein, *Philosophical Investigations* (note 28 to chapter 1), p. 61. Let me add that different languages stress different affinities between various kinds of cognition. For example, a close relationship between "knowing that" and "knowing how" is suggested by the French usage aligning learnable facts (*savoir que*) with the learnable skills of making and doing (*savoir-faire*) or even living (*savoir-vivre*) over against *connaître*—to know or "know of" in the sense of being acquainted. German usage in turn contrasts "knowing that" as *wissen* (etymologically related to an earlier word for "seeing" just as Greek *theoria* is) to being able or "knowing how" and to being acquainted or "knowing of" as *können* and *kennen* (two cognates of the English verb "know").

conversely say that predication is linked in roughly equal measure (rather than lopsidedly) to feeling *and* desire. Let me stress,
however, that I do not wish to elevate predication to the status of
an exclusive paradigm for all cognition. Rather, I concur with
some recent challenges to the cognitive privilege often accorded
to propositional statements about observed objects (e.g., "The cat
is on the mat"). As Nelson Goodman has noted, "Much of knowing aims at something other than true, or any, belief," and as
Lorraine Code suggests from a very different vantage point,
"Knowing other people is at least as worthy a contender for paradigmatic status as knowledge of medium-sized, everyday objects." Goodman's "understanding," associated with "an increase
in acuity of insight," and Code's "second-person" knowledge,
based on day-to-day encounters with other people, highlight two
kinds of significant divergence from the propositional paradigm
for cognition.[17] Their respective arguments provide welcome support for my sense that at least three cognitive paradigms should
be distinguished: one based on phenomenal acquaintance, another on propositional predication, and a third on the practical
prudence associated with both technological and hermeneutic
know-how.[18]

17. See Nelson Goodman, *Ways of Worldmaking* (Indianapolis: Hackett, 1978),
pp. 21–22, and Lorraine Code, *What Can She Know? Feminist Theory and the Construction of Knowledge* (Ithaca: Cornell University Press, 1991), p. 37. Goodman's
nonpredicative examples for the "advancement of understanding" include the
finding of features and structures we could previously not discern in a picture,
concerto, or treatise. Code in turn supports her case as follows: "Developmen-
tally, recognizing other people, learning what can be expected of them, is both
one of the first and one of the most essential kinds of knowledge a child ac-
quires. An infant learns to respond *cognitively* to its caregivers *long before* it can
recognize the simplest of physical objects." Code's observations inadvertently
supplement Stephen E. Toulmin's remarks, quoted above in note 23 to chapter
4, concerning the difference between "knowledge of persons" and "knowledge
of phenomena" as linked to the difference between "expectations of" and "expectations about"; see also Toulmin, p. 314.
18. Husserl's phenomenology, Carnap's logic, and Habermas's "universal
pragmatics" illustrate the predominance of one of the three paradigms in a particular thinker's cognitive endeavors. Within the pragmatic paradigm, the technological "knowing how" to encounter tasks may be distinguished from the

The right side of the chart in turn shows that conation extends, as it were, from reactive inclination (the *desire for* an object or objectified person) through proactive intention (the *desire that* a certain state of affairs be brought about) to interactive participation (a shared *desire with* other people to attain common goals).[19] The fulfillment of reactive inclinations may yield the sweetest individual pleasures of *la dolce vita*, and the realization of shared projects through interactive participation may affect the most noticeable changes in our *vita activa*. But I regard proactive intention as the "central," prototypical phase of conation because it is less one-sidedly dependent on genetically programmed needs or on socially conditioned oughts than are, respectively, "appetitive" inclination and "acculturated" participation.[20] Once again, "prototypical" does not imply "exclusively paradigmatic." The reactive desire *for* something or someone, the proactive desire *that*

---

hermeneutic "knowing how" to encounter human beings. Habermas himself makes the roughly analogous distinction between strategic and communicative actions, respectively oriented toward the agent's success and toward mutual understanding; see his *Theory of Communicative Action* (note 2 to Prologue), 1:75–101 et passim.

19. Lucien Goldmann's example of two people moving a large table as a "transindividual subject" sheds light on participatory volition from the vantage point of neo-Marxist structuralism; see his "Structure: Human Reality and Methodological Concept," in *The Structuralist Controversy*, ed. Richard Macksey and Eugenio Donato (Baltimore: Johns Hopkins University Press, 1970), pp. 101–2. Analytical and postanalytical philosophers have also been exploring what Wilfrid Sellars, *Science and Metaphysics: Variations on Kantian Themes* (London: Routledge, 1968), p. 222 et passim called "we-intentions"; see, e.g., Richard Rorty, *Contingency, Irony, Solidarity* (Cambridge: Cambridge University Press, 1989), chapter 9, and John Searle, "Collective Intentions and Actions," in *Intentions in Communication*, ed. Philip R. Cohen, Jerry Morgan, and Martha E. Pollack (Cambridge: MIT Press, 1990), pp. 401–15.

20. I borrow the contrast between "appetitive" and "acculturated" desires from Gary Watson, "Free Agency," *Journal of Philosophy* 72 (1975): 205–20, reprinted in *Free Will*, ed. Gary Watson (London: Oxford University Press, 1982), esp. pp. 104–6. I should add, however, that the arbitrating self's or ego's deliberate intentions sometimes succeed in bridging the gulf between individual impulse and participatory obligation. They can therefore mediate between Kant's selfish inclination (*Neigung*) and self-transcendent duty (*Pflicht*) or between Freud's pleasure-seeking id and socially imposed superego.

123

such and such become the case, and the transindividual desire *with* other people strike me as distinct, albeit related, conative paradigms.[21]

Each of the three types of awareness can, of course, apply itself recursively as well. Thus each of us can wonder: Must I be pleased that I feel this pleasure? Should I desire to have that desire? May I believe in the reliability of any of my beliefs? Moreover, we seldom decide that a feeling is authentic, a desire desirable, or a belief trustworthy on exclusively self-referential emotive, conative, *or* cognitive grounds. Rather, we typically "cross-examine" our feelings, desires, and beliefs by means of such queries: Do I feel comfortable with this desire or that belief? Should I desire to have such emotive or cognitive experiences? Do I know enough about possible internal and external consequences to cultivate this particular feeling or act upon that particular desire? When a large number of responses to such questions exhibit certain patterns, our fleeting feelings, desires, and beliefs crystallize into the more lasting second-order orientations of attitudes, projects, and worldviews.

To some extent our attitudes, projects, and worldviews remain linked to the first-order matrix of feelings, desires, and beliefs from which they have evolved. This is why we tend to

21. The respective placement of the three "central" forms of awareness (intention, predication, and attention) on figure 2 should make very clear the structural interdependence of conation, cognition, and emotion within the interactive force fields of our natural being *of*, social being *with*, and personal being *toward* the world. Just as proactive intention turns its relative independence from natural and social motivation into a relatively free personal stance toward the world, the prototypical forms of cognition and emotion, too, mediate between two modes of being from the vantage point of a third one represented by the opposite vertex of the triangle of awareness. Less "social" than prudence and less "personal" than acquaintance, every instance of predication claims to re-present a certain "natural" state of affairs; to cite Alfred Tarski's influential example, reprinted from earlier writings in his *Logic, Semantics, Metamathematics* (Oxford: Clarendon, 1956), p. 156: " 'It is snowing' is a true sentence if and only if it is snowing." Analogously, attention to pleasure or pain links each of us—through empathy or sympathy—to the virtual "society" of all centers of emotive awareness capable of experiencing comfort and discomfort.

engage in projects associated with pleasurable feelings, prefer to adopt worldviews in keeping with our desires, and so forth. Yet strong second-order orientations often manage to prompt us to review and evaluate—rather than perpetuate—our biologically, socially, or personally conditioned ways of feeling, desiring, and believing. For example, the heliocentric worldview enabled its adherents to dismiss the long-held belief that the earth was the center of the universe. Likewise, commitment to a project seen as socially beneficial can override personal inclinations; for example, childless citizens occasionally cast ballots for school tax increases contrary to their individual desire for preserving their own affluence. As the three types of our primary and secondary orientations continue to function and develop in tandem, we even learn to apply emotion, conation, and cognition to our personal identity at large, as when we feel pleased with, wish to improve, or make predictions about ourselves.

Needless to say, an individual's attitudes, projects, and worldviews function and develop in constant interplay with the attitudes, projects, and worldviews of other people. The influence of others on a person's evaluative criteria is particularly strong when virtually all people known to him or her seem to share the same emotive tastes, conative goals, and cognitive frameworks. At the other extreme, members of nonhomogeneous societies find themselves pulled in many directions by parental advice, peer pressure, and other kinds of social influence. But individuals in all human societies frequently face the need to take sides— not only for or against their own desires, feelings, and beliefs or their own projects, attitudes, and worldviews, but also for or against the projects, attitudes, and worldviews of other people.

Any instance of such side taking entails the boon and bane of freedom and responsibility discussed in the previous chapter. To spell out the bane—the endless wrestling with "second thoughts"—in terms of the present context: We turn into will-less procrastinators, unfeeling melancholiacs, or dogmatic skeptics if our projects, attitudes, or worldviews are constantly disabled by ever new internal or internalized challenges to them.[22] And there is an opposite danger as well. When certain outcomes of evaluative side taking strike us as no longer challengeable, we may complacently assume that the affirmed project, attitude, or worldview is in complete harmony with the unified will of a community, with the universally shared taste of humanity, or with the deep structure of reality. A person influenced by certain traditions of ethics, aesthetics, or epistemology may verbalize such perceived harmony by ascribing justice, beauty, or truth to the goal of conation, source of emotion, or result of cognition in question. Let me anticipate the ensuing defense of a nonabsolutistic understanding of justice, beauty, and truth by concluding this section with a double-edged assertion: The unfinishable "self-completing" task of individuals, societies, and the human species is hindered both by the hypercritical rejection of all claims of conative, emotive, or cognitive validity and by the uncritically final espousal of any.[23]

## Justice, Beauty, Truth

Justice, beauty, and truth are often assumed to have been the three supreme values of classical Greek culture. Yet no ancient thinker seems to have discussed such a trinity, and the terms in which various Platonic dialogues, for example, extol particular

22. In a conative context, Harry G. Frankfurt (see note 35 to chapter 4), p. 91, characterizes the excessive urge for critical self-evaluation that "leads toward the destruction of a person" as "humanization run wild." He notes that "nothing except common sense and, perhaps, a saving fatigue prevents an individual from obsessively refusing to identify himself with any of his desires until he forms a desire of the next higher order."

23. The expression "self-completing" comes from Clifford Geertz (see note 42 to chapter 1). Here as elsewhere, I take the phrase to stress open-ended progression rather than predetermined destination in the evolution both of individual humans and of our species at large.

values hardly suggest the systematic coordination of a threesome at the same level of supreme worth.[24] To cite just two very obvious examples: According to the *Republic* (4:428–35 et passim), temperance, courage, wisdom, and justice are the four virtues manifested by both the perfect state and the perfect soul, while Diotima's "encomium of love" (*Symposium* 201–12) implicitly touches on several possible candidates for supreme value (e.g., wisdom, beauty, the good, happiness, immortality, virtue, temperance, justice, god).[25] It is easier to justify the triadic coordination of truth, justice (or the ethically good), and beauty as the lodestars of epistemology, ethics, and aesthetics for many philosophers since the publication of Kant's *Critique of Pure Reason* (1781), *Critique of Practical Reason* (1788), and *Critique of Judgment* (1790). But Kant himself laid special stress on the good—conceived as the unselfish doing of one's duty—in the name of the "primacy" of practical reason.[26] Indeed, few—if any—thinkers have ever insisted on the completely equal standing of the three high values. Most would place just one of the three or a fourth (e.g., the holy or sacred) at the top of a value

24. Even the following formulation from Plato's *Phaedrus* falls short of doing that: "The divine is beauty, wisdom, goodness, *and the like*" (246 in Jowett's translation; my italics).

25. It should not be assumed, of course, that Plato's terms were designed to express the concepts that a twentieth-century American reader is likely to associate with them or their English translations. See, for instance, Gregory Vlastos's comments on the ultimately selfish connotations of both Platonic justice and Platonic love: justice (*dikaiosyne*) leads to healthy and pleasurable "psychic harmony" in the just person's soul (*Republic* 4:443–44); love (both as *eros* and as *philia*) emerges as the entranced admirer's pleasurable appreciation of physical or spiritual beauty (*Symposium* 210–12). Vlastos helpfully contrasts Plato's view of love to Aristotle's characterization of loving friendship (*philia*) as one person's altruistic concern for the well-being of another (*Rhetoric* 1380B35–81B1 and *Nicomachean Ethics* 1166A2–5). See "The Individual as an Object of Love in Plato" and "Justice and Happiness in the *Republic*," in Gregory Vlastos, *Platonic Studies* (Princeton: Princeton University Press, 1973), esp. pp. 3–6 and 30–33 (on love) and 111–14 (on justice).

26. See esp. book 2, chapter 2, section 3 of Immanuel Kant, *Critique of Practical Reason*, trans. Lewis White Beck (Indianapolis: Bobbs-Merrill, 1956), pp. 124–26.

pyramid.[27] Some have even suggested that two of the three (e.g., beauty and truth for Keats) are only different aspects of the same highest value.[28]

Proponents of any value as the highest or as deserving nearly equal status with some other supreme value have always needed to combat what they would regard as trivialized versions of it. In their eyes, justice was not to be considered as mere application of a particular set of laws. Nor could the beautiful be exemplified by something so haphazardly agreeable that it pleases me but may legitimately displease you; in part to rule out such contingency, Kant insisted that our appreciation of an object's formal beauty be free of any self-serving "interest" in the actual existence of the object.[29] Likewise, the true had to be sharply distinguished from whatever appears plausible to a particular person or group at a particular time. Especially the good—whether invoked as an alternative concept to justice or as the very principle of worth from which all other values stem—was not to be considered merely instrumental (good for something else). In sum, the just, the beautiful, the true, and the good had to emerge as unconditionally just, beautiful, true, or good in and for themselves.

Such absolutism is quite foreign to the intellectual climate of our day. We tend to think that declaring something either generally good (that is, preferable to its contrary or contradictory) or specifically just, beautiful, or true is the personal expression of a socially conditioned value judgment. That is to say, many of us embrace one version or another of what may be called "perspectival" or "situational" ethics, aesthetics, and epistemology. Yet the original edge of such terms as "perspectival" or "situational" turns quite dull in the widely acknowledged absence of viable

27. See W. M. Urban's article "Value, Theory of," in the 14th edition (1929) of the *Encyclopaedia Britannica* and the literature listed there. The corresponding entry "Axiology" in the first (Micropaedia) volume of the 15th edition (1974, reprinted 1993) is shorter and less informative.

28. See the final lines of John Keats's "Ode on a Grecian Urn."

29. See esp. sections 2 and 3 of Immanuel Kant, *Critique of Judgment* (see note 12 above), pp. 45–48.

absolutist alternatives to perspectivally situated assessments of value. After all, if there is nothing absolute for the relative to be relative to, everything becomes both absolutely relative and relatively absolute.[30] In any event, even the most rigorous adherents to a relativistic theory of value seem to join the rest of us in conducting much of their lives on the basis of assumptions like the following. Some "things done" by and to people are just or at least more just than some others; some vases, horses, and other "things made" by art or nature are beautiful or at least more beautiful than some others; some opinions and other "things meant" are true or at least truer than some others. That is to say, we cannot help but evaluate things done, made, or meant relative to standards that (for the time being) function as good or at least as better than some others.[31]

Figure 3 aligns our evaluations of things done, made, or meant as (more or less) just, beautiful, or true both with the aims of discourse and with the types of awareness mapped in figures 1 and 2. On the conative side, the chart coordinates individual rights and social responsibilities as conjunctively indispensable for ar-

30. In his *Theory and Cultural Value* (Oxford: Blackwell, 1992), Steven Connor proposes to "attempt the difficult feat of thinking absolutism and relativism together rather than as apart and antagonistic." He notes our "irreducible orientation toward the better and revulsion from the worse" and designates it as the "imperative to value." The following sentence from Connor's book may amplify my own ensuing argument for the inevitability, both natural and cultural, of evaluating every instance of human experience: "Neither the suicide who believes that individual annihilation is preferable to continued existence, nor the philosopher who argues that it would have been better for the human race, even for life itself, never to have existed, can resist the imperative of value, even in the apparent denial of all values in particular, since they both depend on the affirmation of and preference for the *better*, even if, as in writers such as Freud, Bataille, and Beckett, the route to the better may seem to lie through the worse" (pp. 1–2).

31. Needless to say, the very assertion that our value judgments are based on socially conditioned personal preference tends to land us in a public or private inquiry as to how good (just, beautiful, and/or true) that assertion and its implications really are. In other words, there is no peremptory closing of the external or mental debate on whether something is absolutely or relatively good and whether something judged to be absolutely or relatively good is good—has value—for this or that ethical, aesthetic, epistemological, and/or other reason.

*Figure 3.* Three directions of evaluation: justice, beauty, truth

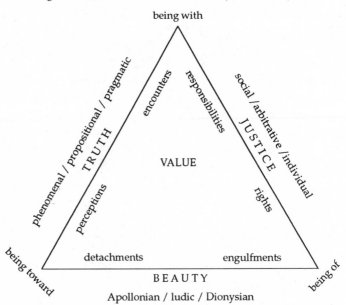

being with

responsibilities

encounters

JUSTICE

social / arbitrative / individual

TRUTH

phenomenal / propositional / pragmatic

VALUE

perceptions

rights

being with

being toward

detachments          engulfments

being of

BEAUTY

Apollonian / ludic / Dionysian

riving at justice through the very arbitration of their conflicting claims.[32] On the cognitive side, the chart coordinates phenomenal perceptions (of objects or people) and pragmatic encounters (with tasks or people) as jointly leading to and gauging the truth of verbalizable propositions. On the emotive south side of the tri-

32. I take "rights" in a broad enough sense to include every individual's right to the fulfillment of such desires as are involved in his or her pursuit of happiness. My notion of responsibility in turn includes the paternalistic bid-dings of Kant's duty and Freud's superego, as well as a more maternal propen-sity for caring and the concomitant sharing of comfort and happiness. Carol Gilligan, *In a Different Voice: Psychological Theory and Women's Development* (Cam-bridge: Harvard University Press, 1982), advocates dialogue between a rights-based "ethic of justice" and a responsibility-oriented "ethic of care," the former proceeding from "the premise of fairness—that everyone should be treated the same" and the latter from "the premise of nonviolence—that no one should be hurt" (see esp. pp. 173–74). If, with Gilligan, one considers rights and responsi-bilities as respectively underlying justice and care, the ethical value resulting from circumspect arbitration among rights and responsibilities might be named "the good" rather than, as it is named in my scheme, "justice."

angle, the chart coordinates world-absorbed engulfment and self-controlled detachment—the intoxicating, carnivalesque rhythms of Dionysian matter and the healing, beatific tranquillity of Apollonian patterns—as reciprocally liberating through aesthetic play.[33]

Likes and dislikes are involved in our cognitive and conative evaluations as well. After all, we find ourselves attracted not only to the perceived beauty of whatever directly triggers certain pleasurable feelings but also to the presumed truth (or at least plausibility) of our beliefs and to the presumed justice (or at least legitimacy) of our desires. For example, we experience a feeling of fulfillment when we solve a puzzle or when a traffic signal stays green long enough for us to cross an intersection. Needless to add, life provides ample occasion for feelings of frustration as well. Even simple chess problems are too tough for most people, and traffic lights tend to turn red before "doing justice" to the desires of all drivers and pedestrians.

In general, many things remain unknown and many desires go ungratified in a pluriverse not made to human specifications. Yet a prudent attitude toward cognition and a participatory attitude toward conation can greatly help in adjusting our emotive gauge for pleasures and displeasures to the sober principle of reality.[34] For example, we can improve our ratio of emotive fulfillment over frustration if we learn to focus on the "truth" of such chess

33. See esp. section 1 of Friedrich Nietzsche, *The Birth of Tragedy*, trans. Walter Kaufmann (New York: Random House, 1967), pp. 33–38, for the characterization of Apollo and Dionysus as "two art-sponsoring deities," and esp. letter 14 of Friedrich Schiller, *On the Aesthetic Education of Man*, trans. Elizabeth M. Wilkinson and L. A. Willoughby (Oxford: Clarendon, 1967), pp. 94–99, for the liberating effect of the "play drive" (*Spieltrieb*) on human beings under the sway of either the "compulsion of nature" or of the "compulsion of reason," respectively manifested by the material "sense drive" (*Stofftrieb*, also called *der sinnliche Trieb*) and the rationally moral "form drive" (*Formtrieb*).

34. The Freudian echo (concerning the "pleasure principle" of spontaneous evaluation and the "reality principle" of cultural adjustment) is intended. For the place of prudently practical knowing and participatory desire among the respective modes of cognition and conation, see the northern tip of figure 2 and the accompanying discussion above.

problems as we can solve and to desire such "justice" as will yield an optimal traffic pattern for people and vehicles approaching the intersection from all directions. By and large, moderation in cognitive and conative pursuits is more likely than excess to make the relationship between the self and its lifeworld a better fit and thereby more harmoniously beautiful. But the strenuous probing of the customary limits of human cognition or conation offers emotive rewards of a different kind when it opens vistas not of circumscribed beauty but of boundless sublimity.[35] For example, both speculative mysticism and utopian politics afford "sublime" combinations of emotive fulfillment and frustration to their respective devotees who, like Goethe's Faust in his dying moments, imaginatively anticipate greater cognitive or conative success than anyone can factually attain.[36]

Since we are frequently pleased or displeased for chiefly cognitive or conative reasons, human evaluations tend to transcend mere biological preoccupation with comfort and discomfort, pleasure and pain. As creators and creatures of culture, we can be profoundly "delighted" through being "taught" or "moved" by other people. Indeed, I know, desire, and feel the way I do in large part because I have been taught, moved, and delighted—or misinformed, demobilized, and abused—by my consociates and by cultural products reaching me across various ranges of geo-

35. See sections 25–29 in Kant's *Critique of Judgment* (see note 12 above), pp. 103–40, on the dynamic and mathematical sublime as respectively related to infinite power and infinite size and for his general definition of the sublime as that which proves that a mind capable of conceiving of it surpasses every standard of sense. See esp. the last difficult sentence of section 25 in Immanuel Kant, *Kritik der Urteilskraft* (see note 12 above), p. 94: "Erhaben ist, was auch nur denken zu können ein Vermögen des Gemüts beweist, das jeden Maßstab der Sinne übertrifft." Kant's juxtaposition of the sublime and the beautiful within what now counts as the aesthetic domain had few precursors (notably Edmund Burke) but many successors.

36. Lines 11,585–86 of Goethe's *Faust* read: "Im Vorgefühl von solchem hohen Glück / Genieß ich jetzt den höchsten Augenblick"; for an English version, see Johann Wolfgang von Goethe, *Faust I and II*, trans. Stuart Atkins (Princeton: Princeton University Press, 1994): "Envisioning those heights of happiness / I now enjoy my highest moment."

graphical or temporal distance.[37] Conversely, the "truth" of my own beliefs and worldviews, the "justice" of my own desires and projects, and the "beauty" of my own embodied feelings and attitudes are constantly tested in social interactions: can I teach, move, or delight you into accepting the offered information, incurring the proposed commitment, appreciating the proffered entertainment? Even my success in doing so remains open to additional evaluation: Have I enlightened or indoctrinated, empowered or co-opted, enriched or seduced you?

One could say in general that an *I* has enlightened, empowered, or enriched (rather than indoctrinated, co-opted, or seduced) some *you* if a joint *we* shall henceforth share any benefit that may accrue from what used to be a particular person's "possession" of truth, justice, or beauty.[38] But the specific determination that such a transformation into *we*ness has indeed occurred must remain subject to further evaluation by *you* and *me* and *them*—engulfed participants as well as more or less detached "third parties" in social interactions. And herein lies the inescapable historicity of all values. Our efforts to teach, move, or delight each other enhance the world's shareable supply of truth, justice, or beauty only insofar as positive responses continue to be forthcoming to queries of the following type: Has the effort in question led to reliable rather than deceptive or self-deceptive

---

37. For some implications of the difference between the world of actual consociates (the peopled *Umwelt* of a person's directly experienced social reality) and the respective larger worlds of our contemporaries, predecessors, and successors (*Mitwelt, Vorwelt, Folgewelt*), see Alfred Schutz, "The Dimensions of the Social World," in *Collected Papers*, 3 vols. (The Hague: Nijhoff, 1962–66), vol. 2, ed. Arvid Brodersen (1964), pp. 20–63.

38. In some cognitive or conative conversions it is hard to determine whether the converter, the convertee, or both should count as benefiting from the interpersonal transaction in question. Furthermore, it is far from clear whether teachers, preachers, movie stars, or professional athletes typically "dominate" their respective audiences or "cater to" them. The student answering questions in an oral or written examination and the stripper performing in a nightclub may serve as rather obvious counterexamples to the supposed rule that the more active participant occupies a position of authority and power in *any* informing or entertaining relationship.

meaning? to mutually enabling rather than suppressive or self-suppressive doing? to harmonious rather than dysfunctional or alienating self- and worldmaking?

## Consensus, Coherence, Correspondence

The following table recapitulates the conceptual links among individual members of the three triads discussed in this chapter. It also anticipates the ensuing consideration of a fourth triad: cultural consensus about desirable interaction, experiential coherence within an embodied mind, and existential correspondence between meaning and being or becoming.

| moving | delighting | teaching |
| willing | feeling | knowing |
| justice | beauty | truth |
| consensus | coherence | correspondence |

The coordination of the last two triads should shed some new light on the entire set of twelve concepts. The alignment of justice with cultural consensus stresses the intersubjective dimension of what moves us to desire justice. The alignment of beauty with experiential coherence in turn explains why a feeling of delight should be triggered by the well-proportioned structure and harmonious functioning both of one's own body and mind and of other products of nature or art. Finally, the alignment of truth with existential correspondence acknowledges the need for continually testing what is believed or taught against what might actually be or become the case. But a historicist understanding of justice, beauty, and truth as values resulting from our ability to move, delight, and teach one another must remain sensitive to three concomitant provisos. In pursuing justice, we must not permit the consensual standards now prevailing among our consociates to narrow our efforts to coordinate individual rights with social responsibilities. In pursuing beauty, we need to realize that harmonious coherence within a particular whole always emerges from incoherence in some of its parts and in its environment. In pursuing truth, we should not forget that circular feedback loops often launder the negative results of cognitive testing until it is too late for the would-be knower's person, society, or species to escape extinction by achieving closer correspondence between cognition and what is being cognized.

Let me elaborate by glancing, for a last time, at evolutionary history. Just as protofeelings of comfort or discomfort begin to register coherence or incoherence within the functioning of increasingly complex organisms, protocognition begins to grasp, and protoconation begins to affect, the environmental conditions for that functioning. Animals on higher rungs of the evolutionary ladder even respond to their experience of comfort and discomfort by modulating some of their "hard-wired" instincts for survival into improvised behavior. For humans, culture replaces nature as the prime motor of evolution because language enables the articulation and exchange of findings on whether certain genes, ideas, and behaviors will typically put us in life-promoting or life-threatening contact with the relevant *Its* and *Thous* of our lifeworlds. Armed with such information, we constantly reassess the degree of coherence in the functioning of our organs (as evinced by feelings of satisfaction), the degree of correspondence between us and the environment (as evidenced by unfalsified beliefs), and the degree of consensus among our consociates (as manifested by mutually affirmed participatory desires).

But if our evolution has enabled us to evaluate in greater depth, our evaluations enable us to evolve at a far more unsettling speed than members of other species. Indeed, each of us is highly susceptible to emotive "growing pains" because the comfortable coherence of well-established *I-It* and *I-Thou* relationships often unravels in the face of our need (and opportunity) to achieve new kinds of cognitive correspondence or conative consensus. To be sure, total emotive coherence in individuals, complete conative consensus in societies, and full cognitive correspondence between the current state of the environment and a particular way of knowing it might result in the evolutionary stagnation of a species incapable of adjusting to radically new challenges.[39] Yet at the other extreme, complete experiential, cultural, or existential incongruence would make human life as we know it altogether impossible. To thrive or at least survive, we need some degree of emotive coherence among our feelings, beliefs, and desires, some degree of conative consensus with our consociates, and some degree of cognitive correspondence between our environment and our ability to know it.

Excessive deficiency in coherence, consensus, or correspondence is likely to lead to mental illness, societal collapse, or specieswide extinction. That is why—and how—natural selection rewards positive attitudes toward individual learning and social cooperation. By definition, even though it is a circular definition, survivors manage to emend their beliefs and communities. Of course we cannot truly know whether we truly know, and no one can unilaterally realize his or her desire for a just society. Thus only nature or society can ultimately "tell" whether a particular attempt at emendation, pleasurably affirmed as such by the individual's reconfigured emotive coherence, has actually led to enhanced cognitive correspondence or conative consensus. Conversely, however, only individuals (rather than nature or society) have those *possibly* true beliefs and *potentially* realizable desires that serve as guides and goals in the natural and social evolution of our "self-completing" species.

39. Some powerful Marxist, Freudian, and existentialist arguments respectively imply that any consensus, coherence, or correspondence must remain illusory until such time (should such time ever come) as social oppression, individual repression, and the natural chasm separating human beings from what Heidegger and Sartre called Being have been eliminated. See esp. Martin Heidegger, *Being and Time* (note 29 to chapter 3), and Jean-Paul Sartre, *Being and Nothingness: An Essay on Phenomenological Ontology*, trans. Hazel E. Barnes (New York: Philosophical Library, 1956). The Marxist and Freudian views just invoked are too well known to require specific citation in the present context.

Since consensus, correspondence, and coherence are continu-ally challenged by diversity in society, nature, and the self, it is im-perative for each of us to possess high thresholds of tolerance for conative, cognitive, and emotive incongruities. Anyone incapable of enduring a fair amount of personal imbalance, cultural discrep-ancy, or epistemic failure will not stay around long enough to en-gage effectively in the interminable individual, social, and evolutionary struggle against them.[40] Different social systems—whether microcommunities like a nuclear family or macroconstel-lations like an entire civilization—foster different kinds and degrees of emotive coherence within individuals by eliciting (or enforcing) different kinds and degrees of conative consensus among them. It is plain that neither oppressive hierarchy nor per-missive anarchy is conducive to developing strong resistance in individuals to both of two opposite mental dangers—ossification and schizophrenia. Indeed, any social formation must undergo change or risk collapse if the kind and degree of conative consen-sus prevailing in it keep too many of its constituent individuals from attaining a vital balance within each psyche between the nec-essary minimum of emotive coherence and the flexibility needed to adjust to newly registered requirements of cognitive correspon-dence and conative consensus.

To be sure, individuals as well as societies have always needed to correlate their ways of processing information about the world with their ways of preparing to intervene in it. Yet the current ex-plosion of technologically efficient know-how imposes on us the immense new task of a worldwide coordination of beliefs with desires, worldviews with projects—indeed, science with moral-

40. My conviction that culture, existence, and experience are too diverse to allow homogenization aligns me, among the English romantics, with Blake rather than Coleridge. Compare, for instance, plate 3 of Blake's *The Marriage of Heaven and Hell* (note 7 to Prologue), p. xvi: "Without Contraries is no progres-sion," with Coleridge's insistence, in chapter 14 of his *Biographia Literaria*, that the imagination is capable of reconciling all "opposite or discordant qualities"; see Samuel Taylor Coleridge, *Biographia Literaria*, ed. James Engell and W. Jack-son Bate (Princeton: Princeton University Press, 1983), 2:16–17.

ity. After all, our predecessors would have been hard put just to imagine our vastly increased power to affect the environment. Topsoil erosion, depletion of crucial mineral reserves, elimination of rain forests, pollution of the oceans and the atmosphere through ill-disposed waste, irreversible genetic engineering, the use of weapons of mass destruction—these are only a few of the many horrors that members of our species can systematically inflict on each other and on countless other species. It is clear that the efficacy of our cognition has jumped ahead of the ethics of our conation and that the race will soon be over unless the laidback moral rabbit manages to catch up with the fervid scientific tortoise.

Beyond doubt, the objective and subjective validity claims of cognitive representations and emotive expressions have always been assessed in the intersubjective dialogue of consociates.[41] Yet we have now reached a precariously unprecedented stage of being human. Our predecessors will not be remembered and our successors will not be born unless we learn to share projects not only with some of our immediate consociates but, in principle, with all contemporaries around the globe. Quite apart from worldwide problems of human health and wealth that can only be addressed cooperatively, it is clear that many governments already have—and some guerrilla leaders may soon have—nuclear and biological weapons at their disposal. Our present historical situation thus calls for very broadly based ethical consensus to determine what kinds of worldviews and attitudes are viable outcomes of the striving for cognitive correspondence and emotive coherence today. But for the long run (if there is to be one), knowledge and feeling must not remain totally eclipsed by desire—not even by a specieswide participatory desire to survive—because no desire can be consistently fulfilled without the relevant knowledge and because no desire is worth fulfilling

41. Cf. Jürgen Habermas, *The Theory of Communicative Action* (note 2 to Prologue), 1:15–16: "The possibility of intersubjective recognition of criticizable validity claims is constitutive for their rationality."

if its fulfillment results in large-scale individual anguish rather than joy. Even in the short run, conative commitments should not be allowed either to blinker our cognitive views of the world or to dismiss our emotive attitudes toward it. Neglect for the cognitive and emotive implications of our projects tends to make us unable even to ask, let alone answer, the three-part question crucial to most collective endeavors: How can power be used altruistically, rebellion constructively, co-optation to mutual benefit?

Now, any particular quest for justice can best moderate its inherent bias against rival quests if it permits itself to be gauged by the cognitive and emotive values of truth and beauty as well. In other words, the conative values of every social practice must be continually checked against the theoretical ideals and personal preferences emerging from it lest a misguided or coerced consensus prevent our cognitive and emotive aspirations from promoting increased correspondence with the natural environment and enhanced coherence within individual experience. Just as we do not want cognition to confine us (in the name of "true" correspondence) to inexorable *I-It* relations, and just as we do not want emotion to reduce us (in the name of "beautiful" coherence) to claustrophobic *I-Me* relations, so too we do not want conation to bind us (in the name of "just" consensus) to constraining *I-Thou* relations either with particular human sisters and brothers or with the Super Ego of an Earth Mother or Heavenly Father. Why should we be confined, reduced, or bound to any singular relation that today's grammar, based on yesterday's rhetoric, projects as first-, second-, or third-personal? I imagine *us*—self-completing humanity's evolving multiple subject of knowledgeably felt desire—ever more avidly searching for something more plural than can appear on any singular horizon, be it the second-person horizon of intersubjective culture, the third-person horizon of objective existence, or the first-person horizon of subjective experience. Thanks to such searching, our social, natural, and personal modes of simultaneously being

139

with, of, and toward our surrounds may well be on the verge of enabling us to desire, feel, and know what is at once within and beyond all existing ways of doing, making, and meaning: nontripartite diversity.

# Epilogue:
# Loose Ends and Afterthoughts

Much more occurs to each of us than can be voiced in a single persona. This is why a great deal of mental discussion goes on even as we prepare to speak our minds. The following conversation recaptures some of what I overheard about the present book while it was, as the saying goes, in progress. But I am not sure how many distinct voices are recorded here and whether they mainly convey anticipated critiques of the book or internal challenges to it.

—My biggest complaint about *Cultural Transactions* is that the book tries to cover too much without spelling out what it tries to discover.

—That's funny. I was going to say just about the opposite. I guess I must be less happy with Hernadi's coverage than with his discoveries.

—How so?

—For one thing, he should have acknowledged more often that other authors may be barking up some of the same trees. For example, just one passing reference to Foucault and two or three to Gadamer are hardly enough to indicate what he has learned from them about, say, authorship and tradition.

—You can't quote everything you've read.

—Of course not. Who wants to be reminded that our minds, like Arcimboldo's "Librarian," are mostly made up of books by other people? But I'm not even sure Hernadi has read with sufficient care everything he does quote. Take the Searle/Derrida debate about speech acts. At one point . . .

—Never mind the details, that's the devil's stomping ground in any case. What I want to know is how Hernadi fares with the angels. Do they have enough space to spread their wings in his trinitarian worlds of doing, making, and meaning?

—I can't vouch for the angels. Let me say, though, that I rather like the open-ended way he both aligns and contrasts those triads upon triads: speaking, writing, thinking; communication, expression, representation; society, nature, individuality; and so forth.

—Don't forget the old staple: justice, beauty, and truth.

—Rather newfangled, that one, if you relate it to Hernadi's last triad: cultural consensus, experiential coherence, and existential or environmental correspondence.

—Well, yes—some of the stuff is quite clever. But on the whole I find his scheme of schemes too seamless. For instance, when he suggests that culture, existence, and experience emerge from each other I'm reminded of the Escher drawing where two hands sketch one another. A good visual joke, perhaps, but don't we know all the while that Escher drew both hands?

—Sure. Just as Michelangelo created both Adam and his— whose?—Creator for the ceiling of the Sistine Chapel. If you ask me, Adam's outstretched arm transfuses the painter's human life into the bearded old gent even as His pointing finger transfuses divine life into Adam.

—I see. You want to have your myth and eat it too. As for me, I'm ready to descend from painted ceilings to the quaking earth.

—To each his own taste.

—Or hers, I should hope. Which reminds me: Hernadi often calls the worlds he surveys human. So why does he hide, like a transcendent God, behind his universal interplay of culture, existence, and experience? I would have liked to hear a lot more about *his* culture, existence, and experience: Who occupies center stage and who gets marginalized in them? I suppose you folks don't care what prompts Hernadi to do, make, and mean the kinds of things he does, makes, and means.

—Wrong again. I too wish he were exposing more of his roots. He's critical of capitalism but seldom sounds like a socialist. He says he's Hungarian, but isn't he also Jewish? Even his concluding the book with our dialogue about it is a ploy to hide himself: a bunch of us are made to converse so that he can convey his afterthoughts without appearing to do so.

—Are you accusing him of willful deception?

—Not quite. But only because he knows no one will be fooled. How could we, denizens of an epilogue to the first edition, talk about the book as if we'd read it? Even so, I'm troubled by this kind of playful evasion. Hernadi shouldn't leave it to others to relate his text to its historical context.

—Why on earth not? I'm getting tired of authors who "situate" their position into the ground. Are they trying to make us forget that any such situating can in turn be situated? After all, any . . .

—I bet you're about to proclaim that even the most thorough definition of one's own ideological bias can be challenged from the outside as ideologically biased.

143

—I'm glad you don't seem to need such a reminder. Let me say, though, that I for one don't mind letting our reader wonder just whose (and how many) voices we are. The usual alternative is for all of us to chant in the docile unison of a single authorial choir, and I don't wish to be effectively silenced that way.

—Me neither. But can I be sure that your voice isn't being raised to cancel mine by preserving it as a "sublated" thesis or antithesis within your co-optive synthesis? For all I know, you may just be a front for Hernadi's overarching dialectic of Hegelian *Aufhebung*.

—Look who's talking! Hasn't our self-effacing author just used your last speech to remind his reader of the German origin of "sublation" and its triple meaning: lift up, cancel, and preserve?

—Stop fussing, both of you! What's the point in endlessly suspecting each other of hegemonic sublation? Instead, we should pledge joint allegiance to the counterpoint of diversity.

—And declare war on the premature harmony of synthesis?

—OK by me. The very sound of "sublation" has always reminded me of subjugation. Don't you see? All synthesis writ large reflects the will to dominate. We must fight the deadly syn of dialectic pride and nurture the humble virtue of polythesis.

—Writ large? I guess one can't be humble enough when fighting the pride of an other.

—Cute.

—You mean embarrassing?

—Not really, because my idea of polythesis entails that all theses, antitheses, and even syntheses (writ small) are enabling prerequisites of each other. As the fourth principle, polythesis is just another name for radical diversity: it challenges all unifying principles including itself, should it turn out to be one. Therefore . . .

—You sound more and more like Hernadi when he tries to reduce the concrete realities of nature, society, selfhood, and diversity to such "principles"—and he writes them large—as the One as Many, the Many as One, the One as One, and the Many as Many. Very abstract principles indeed.

—Abstract, shmabstract! Fundamental ideas like one and many are quite down to earth. Especially by comparison, I don't see how you can think of nature, society, selfhood, or diversity as "concrete." Has anyone ever broken a bone bumping into one of them?

—Look, I'm not in the mood to revive the age-old dispute between empiricists and rationalists. But if you claim that my empirical sense of concrete reality is all in the mind, I have news for you: ideas must be experienced in material brains to count as rational. Besides, all concepts and all theoretical frameworks emerge from and recede into the historical process.

—I grant you that. But let's not forget that "material brain" is a concept and that any and all "historical process"—namely, what changes, how, and why—can be theorized in many different ways. In fact, what you call concrete historical reality can't emerge, and certainly can't reach consciousness, except within the grids of what you call abstract theories and ideas.

—Listening to you guys makes me realize we're still in the grip of such traditional binaries as rationalism versus empiricism and idealism versus materialism. Some of us have simply transposed those oppositions into the more fashionable one of theory versus history.

—If that's correct, I must really fault Hernadi. He should have made more of an effort both to uncover such parallels and to illuminate significant differences between them. Instead, he

145

tends to outflank entrenched positions just when I wish he would attack or defend them.

—Right on. I particularly resent that he assimilates the work of scholars like Carol Gilligan and Lorraine Code to the mainstream—malestream—tradition. If not *he, we* certainly cherish their feminist edge. And as Hernadi occasionally admits, our talking and listening to each other has not yet reached a stage at which it shouldn't matter who says "we" to whom and about whom. On the other hand . . .

—Escher's two hands again?

—On the other hand, I don't object to the project of achieving what Hernadi calls the "ecumenical we." I only insist on the present plurality of *wes,* on the word's and the world's current unresolved dialectic of inclusion and exclusion. And I'm greatly troubled by Hernadi's tendency to imply that his Utopia—the social, natural, and personal intertwining of the diverse—is just around the corner.

—I didn't get the impression that he thinks we're about to enter a promised land of universal *we*ness. Nor did I catch him suggesting that our "being with" other people will soon mean just "being for" (without also "being against") them. What he does seem to propose is this: Our differences keep being transformed while individual identity, social activity, and natural facticity—*I, You,* and *They*—are becoming intertwined in diverse ways.

—Does that mean that in human worlds, as in our conversation of disembodied voices about them, intertwining and diversity can remain at once diverse and intertwined?

—I couldn't have put it better. Let me just elaborate on what you've said by linking the three pronominal perspectives to one of Hernadi's other schemes of being human. Each of us is an *I* turning *toward* the world, a *You* interacting *with* the world, and an *It* existing as one of many building blocks *of* the world.

But our being toward, being with, and being of the world are distinguishable only by virtue of their being intertwined. After all, the difference between being of the world of perceivable and categorizable *Its* and being with the world of competing and cooperating *Yous* presupposes a distinguishing *I*'s awareness of its own being toward two different kinds of worlds and vice versa.

—Listening to you just now makes me really wonder: Are you speaking about Hernadi's book or is he speaking, in your ventriloquized voice, for it?

—That makes two of us, because listening to *you* makes *me* wonder whether your raising such an antagonistic question isn't the most surreptitious way of speaking for the book and for its author.

—Why would you say that?

—Don't you remember the last paragraph of the Prologue? Hernadi expects his own image to be drawn into any picture that his critics might draw or frame of the arguments he's been framing. Now that he has drawn our critical remarks into his picture, he is sure to claim that whatever we say simply enacts the past and future of his book from his memory and imagination.

—Can't we retort that it's he who's been plagiarizing us and other voices from his memory and imagination all along?

—Hey, such a claim may even earn us some royalties on the book!

—Don't bank on it because . . . because . . . Yes, I feel it coming.

—Me too. He's about to conclude both the book and this conversation by making me misquote Matt. 18:20 to the effect that whenever two or three are gathered together in his frame, there he is in the midst of them.

# Index

The alphabetized entries of the general index are followed by separate listings of some triads and tetrads in the order of their first appearance.

Williams, Raymond, 86n12
Wimsatt, W. K., 14n10
Winnicott, D. W., 83n5
Wittgenstein, Ludwig, 23, 59n25,
121n16
Wittig, Monique, 76n28
Wordsworth, William, 40n5, 114
World, 29n37, 33, 75, 146, 147; hetero-
chronous character of, 54; plurality
of, 1, 4, 105. *See also* Worlds
World-making, 2, 11, 12n9
Worlds, 12n9, 33, 73n24, 74, 80. *See
also* World, plurality of
Worldview, 31, 137, 138
Wurtzler, Steve, 50n17

You, 2, 22, 60, 63, 73, 83, 84n7; plural
of, 63, 79, 80; and Ross Perot's use
of, 60, 62; and thou, 135; and we,
68, 146

Zeno, 92n24
Zeuxis, 44

TRIADS

Culture, existence, experience: and
culture, nature, personal identity,
2, 18, 19n21; and diversity, 79, 105;
and freedom, 104, 107; interdependence of, 142; and link to other
triads, 1, 108, 109; and technology,
34; and time, 54; and we, 3n2
Doing, making, meaning: and action,
production, signification, 55, 57;
and aims of rhetoric, 109–110; and
art and architecture, 50; and cinema, 45; as dimensions of discourse, 7–34; and freedom versus
determinism, 103; and games, 35;
and link to other triads, 1, 108–109,
142; and relativism, 129; and role of
in evolution, 22; social problems
associated with, 28; and technology, 34; and we, 2
Being with, being of, being toward:
and awareness, 120, 124n21; and
diversity, 105–106, 140; and feeling

and desire, 119; and link to other
schemes, 29n37; and link to other
triads, 108; and plural worlds, 1;
and pronominal perspectives,
146–147; simultaneity of, 33; and
value, 120; and we, 75, 79, 84n7
Roles, organisms, persons or selves,
1, 3, 10, 33, 79, 108
Second-, third-, first-person orientations: in all languages, 73; and
communicative, expressive, referential functions, 22; dialectic interplay of, 2, 3, 74,146–147; and fourth
and fifth person orientations,
65–66n10; link to other triads, 33,
108; referents of, 63; and we, 5, 75,
78–79, 83
Activity, facticity, identity, 2, 10, 74,
103, 106, 146; and link to other
triads, 108; and relationship to
aims of rhetoric, 110, 111
Speaking, writing, thinking: and
analogues in the arts, 49; and
Cartesianism, 31–32; changing
functions of, 37; as doing, making,
meaning, 7–21; and links to other
triads, 108, 142; in postliterate
society, 25–28, 33, 38; and time, 53;
and we, 74
Society, nature, self (social, natural,
individual or personal): and Cartesianism, 31; and evolution, 5,
98n33; and freedom, 99, 100, 103,
104, 106, 107; and dialectical interplay, 6, 118, 139, 142, 146; and
diversity, 3, 79, 80–81, 105, 139; and
Mead, George Herbert, 86; and the
multiple self, 19n21, 125; and time,
53–54
Consensus, congruence or correspondence, coherence, 3, 33, 109,
134–140; and relationship to other
triads, 134, 142
Intersubjective, objective, subjective
dimensions: and architecture, 50;
and culture, existence, experience,
138, 139; and different worlds,